The Game Cook

the Game cook

*Recipes inspired by a conversation
in my butcher's shop*

Norman Tebbit

With illustrations by Debby Mason

GRUB STREET · LONDON

This revised and updated edition published in 2017 by

Grub Street

4 Rainham Close

London, SW11 6SS

Email: food@grubstreet.co.uk

Web: www.grubstreet.co.uk

Twitter: @grub_street

Facebook: Grub Street Publishing

Reprinted 2017

A CIP catalogue record for this book is available from the British Library.

ISBN 978-1-910690-44-4

Printed and bound by Finidr, Czech Republic

Contents

Acknowledgements

TO THE LATE Beryl Goldsmith, who typed every page of the book, mostly several times over; the Aylings, father and son, of the New Street Butchers, Horsham; Michel George for some of the fish recipes and whose Belgian connections imported the recipe for rabbit with prunes; Jeremy Ashpool of Jeremy's Restaurant, Borde Hill, who contributed one of his favourite venison recipes; Debby Mason, my illustrator, who also contributed some of her recipes (all Debby's recipes are marked DM), my daughter Alison who checked mine; and all my shooting friends who have helped me provide the birds and beasts for these recipes.

Inspiration:
game in the kitchen

THIS BOOK WAS inspired by a conversation in my favourite butcher's shop. I commented that I noticed that many people bought rubber-boned, tasteless chicken in supermarkets rather than good-quality pheasants for less. 'Why do they do it?' I asked. 'They even pay twice the price if the label on the poor creature says "organic" or "free range". And surely the life of a game bird is better than that of such chickens?'

'Mostly', said the butcher 'because they have never cooked game. They think it is difficult, tastes strange and they wouldn't like it.' The more I thought about it and the more people I asked, the more I believed he was right. We tried putting photocopies of my favourite ways of cooking pheasants on his counter and found they helped to sell pheasants.

I decided to write about game. Not only about cooking it but also about game itself, and why it is good food. As for the cooking, well cooking is not a science. I enjoy cooking and it should not be a chore. I am a great admirer of Delia Smith's cookbooks. If you have never even boiled an egg, stand to attention, open her book and briskly (without hesitation or deviation) do exactly as she orders, and even complicated recipes turn out well. I admire Jane Grigson too. As for her daughter, Sophie, I am also a fervent fan.

I have tried to steer a middle course between these titans of the kitchens. These recipes will work if you follow them, but they are not sacred texts. I hope you will try them – then vary them and make them your own, and there is room at the end of the book for your own notes. My own cookery books are covered in notes – 'needs more cream' or 'double the amount of chutney'.

I should make it plain that I learned only basic cooking at my mother's knee. Then in my airline flying days I was often away for two or three weeks at a time, then at home for a week or more. When I was at home I shared domestic duties with my wife, who taught me to be a more adventurous cook. For the past thirty-three years, since Sinn Fein/IRA terrorists almost murdered us both and left her crippled, I have been the family cook – assisted by advice from the wheelchair.

My gurus of the kitchen have been the Grigsons – Jane and Sophie – Carrier and, of course, Delia Smith. No kitchen should be without Delia's *Complete Illustrated Cookery Course* or Sophie Grigson's *Meat Course, Fish Course* and *Eat Your Greens.* Jane Grigson's *English Food,* Elizabeth David's *French Provincial Cooking* and Joyce Molyneux's *Carved Angel Cookery Book* should also be on the shelf, and for fun, the *Two Fat Ladies: Gastronomic Adventures* (whose fish pie is the greatest).

With a few exceptions (mayonnaise and soufflés, for example), you should not have to stick precisely to quantities. My recipe for pheasants and cream is just one of hundreds of variations on that classic dish. Make it the way that pleases you. Try it with Cointreau rather than

Calvados, green or red apples, peeled or not, and have a glass of Sancerre for the cook along the way.

Enjoy cooking as well as eating. Enjoy this book as much as I have enjoyed experimenting in the kitchen and writing it.

The illustrations are by Debby Mason, who created the mezzotint plates from which they were printed. Sometimes called 'half tone', mezzotints were invented by Ludwig von Siegen in the 17th century. Mezzotints are produced on copper plates. The entire surface of the plate is roughed with a tool, shaped like a wide chisel with a curved and serrated edge – the Mezzotint Rocker. By rocking the toothed edge backwards and forwards over the plate, a rough burr is cast up which holds the ink. Once completed, a drawing can be transferred onto the plate, using carbon paper. When printed, this textured ground reads as a uniform dark; the areas to be lightened are scraped and burnished – therefore working from dark to light.

The preparation of the plate can take 15 hours or more before the artist can start work on the design, but the beautiful, soft velvety finish is so unique to the mezzotint process that it more than justifies the skill and patience involved. In the 18th century, small boys were employed to 'rock' the plates up and the extreme tediousness of the work, combined with the poor pay and working conditions, sent many of the poor things into mental decline, hence the term 'off one's rocker'.

So what is game?

STRICTLY SPEAKING, game is any animal, bird or fish living wild that is hunted for food. By convention, game is divided into three categories: small birds, such as quail, then birds such as grouse, partridge, pheasant and duck, as well as rabbit and hare, and finally larger game, which includes deer, wild boar and in some parts of the world, bear.

Of course, most of us would not share the Mediterranean passion for killing and eating songbirds, and if you want to roast a bear you are on your own as far as I am concerned. What is more, although most partridges and pheasants are not fully wild, in that they are protected by gamekeepers and may be hatched in pens before release into the wild, they are neither kept captive in sheds nor slaughtered like Bernard Matthews' turkeys at the end of their brief lives.

The secret of the superior texture and flavour of game is that the creature has lived as a fully-functional wild animal. They are not dosed with food and confined to a pen or a shed. Although pheasant in particular often have the benefit of food being supplied by their keepers, that is as much to keep them from wandering off on to someone else's land as to feed them. They are free to (and need to) forage for their own food. If you can distinguish between the rubber de-beaked chicken that has never seen sunshine, been showered by rain or felt grass under its feet before its life ended at six weeks or less, and a 'free-range' bird confined to a yard outside its barn, then you will certainly appreciate the meat of a bird that has flown, and run free through woods and fields. And what a difference there is between those pallid, long, frozen Chinese rabbits and the real thing that has lived, loved and feasted on my roses or my farming friends' carrots.

I am not too sure that I would be able to tell the difference between top-quality farmed venison and the truly wild meat, so do not lightly refuse to use the farmed variety if the wild is not on your butcher's slab.

Traditionally, game excludes fish – despite the expression 'game fish'. This book does not take quite such a narrow view. Anyway, almost all the fish we eat is wild and has been hunted and caught – and very good it is too – but I have confined my recipes to those for that fish of fish, the salmon – and I have also included scallops because my illustrator, Debby Mason, goes scuba diving for them, as well as crabs and mackerel. In short, for me, to be game it must have lived free, been hunted or trapped, hooked or shot, whether it be feathered, furred or scaly, or in a shell.

These days you may well find game on the shelves of your supermarket, and it may well be (particularly at Waitrose) of decent quality and reasonable price. My advice, however, is to find a good butcher, get to know him, tell him what you want, trust his judgement – and never forget to tell him if what you bought was good or bad.

Useful tips

Servings

All the recipes serve 4 unless otherwise indicated.

Kit for the kitchen

I am sure that almost every reader will have their own
favourite pieces of kitchen equipment and I would not
want to tell anyone how to equip their kitchen – but there
are some things that you really need to make game cooking
easy. These are my favourite and much-used items:

* A really good-quality 25-28cm/10-11in double-handled, stainless-steel pan – about 10cm/4in deep with a
  well-fitting lid.
* Two large 25-28cm/10-11in frying pans, one stainless
  steel and one coated. I do not use coated pans a lot
  (for one thing you cannot scrape at them with a
  stainless-steel fish slice) but now and again they are
  really useful.
* At least one smaller stainless-steel frying pan.
* It always pays to buy the best-quality casserole pans
  and I do not think there are any better than Le
  Creuset. I have a couple of round ones – 20cm/8in –
  and a couple of oval ones – 28cm/11in x 23cm/9in.
  The lids fit so well and they hold heat very well, and

like stainless-steel pans they are easy to clean. (If for any reason your pans have lids that do not fit tightly, use a piece of kitchen foil under the lid to seal in all the moisture so that it doesn't evaporate.) Nor would I like to be without my Le Creuset griddle.

* Then there is a roasting tin, a good rack for it and several of those lightweight coated baking sheets or very shallow baking trays (about 5mm/¼in). I also have a large and a smaller brown earthenware casserole.

* Amongst the odds and ends, I value my poultry scissors, three or four wooden spoons, a good stainless-steel fish slice and a couple of plastic fish slices to use on coated surfaces.

* I also have a good selection of knives.

I realise that our kitchen is very well equipped, but it has taken my wife and I over fifty years and goodness knows how much money to build it up. Our advice to anyone starting from scratch is to buy the best – and if you cannot afford that, buy something cheap (then, when you can afford the good article, you will not feel bad about throwing the old one out or using it in the garden shed). The mistake is to spend almost as much as the best would cost and feel it is not good enough – but also feel that it cost too much to throw out.

As ever, Peter Jones – or other John Lewis Group shops – offer excellent value and good quality, mainly in the south of England, and the mail catalogues are good value for the cheap and cheerful stuff.

Planning ahead

Many of the recipes here are roasts, and one of the perennial problems with a roast, apart from making sure that the joint and any trimmings, plus all the vegetables, are ready at the same time, is making sure that you have hot serving dishes and plates to hand when you need them. As soon as the meat is carved it will start to cool, and if it is then put on to cold plates, even hot gravy will not be enough to redeem the sorry situation. To avoid this, plan ahead. If you have a range cooker, then the warming oven will be perfect. If you have a double oven, the main oven can be set high for the roast and the second oven on a lower heat for the plates and dishes. Things get more complicated when you have just one oven. If you take the joint out of the oven to rest before carving, leave the oven door slightly ajar to reduce the heat and put plates and dishes inside to warm. If all the food is coming out of the oven at the same time, then be resourceful: fill a clean sink with boiling water and immerse the plates in that; put them in the microwave (if they are microwave-proof); use a microwave-heated plate warmer; stand them on a heat tray...

Jointing a pheasant or partridge

The structure of most game birds is just the same as that of a chicken. Ducks and geese I still find a bit puzzling when I am carving, as the legs are designed as much for swimming as for walking but, with only a little swearing, I usually get it about right. The main thing is not to be intimidated either by the bird itself or the kitchen bystanders, who should be told to go and do the washing up – or pour the cook a glass of wine.

You do need a sharp knife – not too long – I would suggest about 10-15cm/4-6in, and a pair of poultry scissors or shears. My mother's father, who was a butcher, maintained that you are far more likely to cut yourself using a blunt knife than a sharp one and I think he was right.

Always start with the bird on its back on a good wooden board. The first thing to do is to remove the legs. If you simply hold the bird firmly down on to the board with one hand and pull a leg out and down away from the body with the other, you will feel where the top joint (the hip) joins the main skeleton, and if it is a young and tender one you may feel the hip joint dislocate. Cut down through the stretched skin and the knife will more or less find its own way down to the joint. A little pressure and you will find yourself through the meat and looking at the joint. Press the leg out again and the joint will fully dislocate. Flushed with success, cut down through the rest of the skin and meat, and put the first leg to one side. Now turn the bird around and do the same again.

Next, slide your knife down along the breastbone to separate it from the meat on one side of the bone. With a bit of practice you will find this quite easy (and you will leave less and less meat on the breast bone). Continue separating the breast meat right down from the ribs and the backbone. Turn the bird around and separate the other breast. You have now got four pieces: two legs and two breasts with the wings attached.

On a chicken your next move would be to remove the bony little outer winglets with the scissors or shears. Very often you will find that they have been removed when the bird was plucked. Indeed, there is not a lot of meat on a partridge or small pheasant wing, and the plucker may have already removed them. Sometimes most of one wing may have gone if it took a heavy load of shot, came down heavily or was retrieved by an over-enthusiastic Labrador.

Trim the parson's nose off the carcass. Now to make six pieces you will need to divide each breast. This is a matter of judgement to get a fair division between a smaller piece of breast with the leg (which does not have much meat on it) and a larger piece of just breast.

Stock

There are quite a lot of myths about making stock. However, stock as used in the recipes in *The Game Cook* are really quite simple and straightforward. The ingredients are quite variable according to whether you are making stock from the carcasses of game birds, or from those of rabbits, hares or deer.

The basic method is to bring the carcass and any giblets (kidneys, liver etc.) and some vegetable pieces (onion, carrot, celery etc.) some herbs (parsley, thyme, basil, tarragon) and seasoning (salt, black pepper and peppercorns) together in a saucepan with about 1.2 litres/2 pints of cold water per bird and rather more according to size for the rabbit etc. Bring it all up to the boil quite briefly with the lid on the pan, then turn down to simmer for 30 minutes.

Any spare stock can be frozen for later use. I find that containers in which one makes ice cubes are useful and I turn the cubes out and keep them in a freezer bag.

Pheasant, partridge, pigeon stock:

The carcass and any bits of
   one bird
1.2 litres/2 pints water
6 black peppercorns
3 twigs of fresh thyme or

1 tsp dried thyme
3 sprigs of parsley
Other herbs – basil,
   tarragon etc. to taste
Salt, to taste

Break the carcass into two or three pieces. Put in the saucepan with the herbs and seasoning. Bring to the boil, then turn down to a simmer with the lid on for 30 minutes. Strain the stock into a suitable container and discard the remainder.

Rabbit, hare or venison stock:

The carcass, with heart, liver
   and/or kidneys if not
   used elsewhere
1.3 litres/2¼ pints cold water
6-12 black peppercorns
   according to the size of

the carcass
6 twigs of fresh thyme
6 sprigs of parsley
Other herbs, basil and
   especially tarragon, to
   taste

Place all the ingredients in the cold water in a covered pan. Bring briefly to the boil then turn down to simmer for 45 minutes to one hour according to the size of the carcass of bones. Strain the stock into a suitable container and discard the remainder.

Beurre manié

A beurre manié is simply a paste of equal amounts of butter and flour. All you do is soften the butter over a low heat in a saucepan, add the flour a little at a time, and mix to a really stiff paste with a wooden spoon. It needs to be a bit softer than Blu-Tack.

You will not often need very much and I suggest that unless a recipe calls specifically for more, you should use no more than 50g/2oz each of flour and butter. Usually you will be adding this to stock, sauce or gravy to thicken it so I would add it in lumps about thumbnail size.

Some recipes will suggest you use onion as well as the butter and flour. In this case cut about 50g/2oz of onion into very thin slices. Fry gently until soft in 50g/2oz of butter and then add the flour as above.

Bouquet garni

This is just a handy way of using herbs to add flavour without leaving stalks of thyme, bedraggled-looking parsley or bay leaves in the dish. You could cheat and buy a packet of bouquet garni consisting of mixed dried crushed herbs in bags like tea bags.

The other way is to decide on what fresh herbs would go best in the dish you are preparing – very often thyme, coriander, parsley, basil and oregano. Cut fairly long stalks of them (4cm/2in or so), wrap around with a bay leaf and tie firmly together with string around the bay leaf.

Mashed potato and celeriac

Don't use anything but good potatoes, King Edwards, Maris or the like, and choose your celeriac carefully. There can be a lot of waste when you peel it and if you get an old or not very fresh one you may find the centre a bit fluffy. If so discard those bits. However, it is best if you keep reasonably near to a ratio of twice as much celeriac to potato.

450g/1lb potatoes
900g/2lb celeriac
2-3 garlic cloves, according
   to taste

150ml/¼ pint thick cream
50g/2oz butter
Salt and pepper to taste

Peel the potatoes. Dice them into 2cm/1in cubes and put into a saucepan of cold water. Similarly peel the celeriac, discarding the root pieces and any 'fluffy' bits in the centre. Dice it into 2cm/1in cubes and put in a saucepan of cold water.

Then drain off both potatoes and celeriac, give them fresh water and cook in separate saucepans, bringing them to the boil then turning them down to a fast simmer (adding the garlic to the potatoes). This should take about 10 minutes. You will want them soft but not mushy.

When cooked put them together in a good large bowl big enough to use a hand-held electric mixer in. Start to mix them and as the lumps break up chop the butter into bits and add it and the cream. Continue to mix until you get a nice smooth paste.

Conversion tables

If you are of my generation, you are probably still attached to the old imperial measurements that served us and the Americans so well (but watch out for the American gallon – it is a poor, skinny thing, 20 per cent smaller than ours). In my old days as a civil airline pilot, I found myself working in feet as well as metres – but fortunately almost everything was in nautical miles (rather longer than statute miles) and uplifting fuel (which I had calculated in pounds then converted to gallons or litres, remembering that the volume of a pound of fuel varies according to temperature), so I became adept at holding in my mind some very rough and ready conversion factors, which helped to avoid making a truly ghastly error.

It is not a bad idea to have some of these in mind in the kitchen when we find ourselves mixing imperial and metric units – for example, a pint is a bit more than half a litre, a pound a bit less than half a kilo, and 200°C is 400°F. By tradition we measure small volumes by the spoonful. That is fine, except that in my kitchen drawer teaspoons are all different sizes. However, I stick by two teaspoons to a dessert spoon and three teaspoons to a tablespoon. Traditionally it is two tablespoons to a fluid ounce (remember there are twenty fluid ounces to the pint).

So, although the tables opposite should be useful, I hope you will not have to turn to them too often – although I do for oven temperature conversions.

Volume

1 teaspoon	5ml	20fl oz (1 pint)	570ml
1 tablespoon	15ml	1¾ pints	1 litre
5fl oz (¼ pint)	150ml	2 pints	1.2 litres
10fl oz (½ pint)	300ml	4 pints	2.25 litres
16fl oz (¾ pint)	450ml		

Weight

½oz	12g	8oz (½lb)	225g
1oz	25g	10oz	275g
2oz	50g	12oz (¾lb)	350g
3oz	80g	1lb	450g
4oz (¼lb)	115g	2¼lb	1kg
6oz	175g		

Oven temperatures

110°C	225°F	Gas Mark ¼
120°C	250°F	Gas Mark ½
140°C	275°F	Gas Mark 1
150°C	300°F	Gas Mark 2
170°C	325°F	Gas Mark 3
180°C	350°F	Gas Mark 4
190°C	375°F	Gas Mark 5
200°C	400°F	Gas Mark 6
220°C	425°F	Gas Mark 7
230°C	450°F	Gas Mark 8
240°C	475°F	Gas Mark 9

'Like all game you will
not find much fat on
a pheasant – certainly
not until around
Christmas after they
have been stuffing
themselves with
acorns'

Pheasant

Phasianus colchicus

Pheasant, 26

Pheasant with apples and cream, 28

Pheasant with red cabbage, 31

Easiest-ever curried pheasant
with dhal, 33

Roast pheasant, 36

Simple casseroled pheasant, 40

Pheasant with pigs' trotters, 42

Pheasant with brown rice, 45

Pheasant

Season (UK): 1st October–1st February

THE PHEASANT IS by far the most familiar and the most popular game bird in Britain, although it is not a true native. Certainly it was brought here before the Norman Conquest, perhaps by the Romans, and it is now found everywhere except for the far north-west of Scotland.

A good well-grown cock bird may have a wingspan of 90cm/3ft and weigh 1.3kg/5lb or more. Although pheasants are well able to survive anywhere that they can find seeds, grain shoots and acorns for food, cover for their ground nests and good roosting spots on the edges of woods, their natural population is hugely increased by the release in the spring of young birds that have been raised and protected by gamekeepers.

Such is the popularity of shooting that the price received by shoot managers falls as low as 50 pence per bird. Before the Second World War, in a comment on the financial folly of raising pheasants, it was said that 'up goes half a crown (12½pence – the cost of rearing a bird), bang goes sixpence (2½pence – the cost of shooting it) and down comes a shilling (5 pence – the value of the dead bird)'. These days it is more like 'up goes £20, bang goes 50p and down comes £1'. The beneficiary is the customer, who should be able to buy a good pheasant, plucked and cleaned, for anything from £3.50.

My own butcher sells boned, stuffed, oven-ready birds for around £6.50.

Once you have your bird in the kitchen, note that anything you can do with a chicken you can do with a pheasant – and then some. Unlike a chicken, a pheasant (and almost all game) does need to be hung for its flesh to tenderise and the full flavour to develop. That presents some problems these days, as our masters in Brussels and Whitehall decree that once shot, your game birds must be kept in a cooler at a temperature no higher than 4°C/40°F. At that temperature it needs at least ten days before the bird is cleaned. Oh – and do not worry about lead shot: it rarely stops in the flesh of the bird and if it does it will not poison you. Bottom-feeding water fowl are at risk because lead pellets accumulate in their crops – but humans do not have crops so the lead does not hang around in our digestive system.

As with all game you will not find much fat on a pheasant – certainly not until around Christmas after they have been stuffing themselves with acorns – so I generally casserole rather than roast them. As ever, cooking a bird in a casserole could not be more straight-forward, but it is the quality of fruit, vegetables, other meats, wine, cider and spirits that turn a decent bird into a magnificent meal.

Pheasant with apples and cream

Phaisan à la Normande

THIS IS MY FAVOURITE way of cooking pheasant. It is a classic casseroled dish that depends not just on the quality of the bird but also on the fruit, vegetables and other ingredients used. A good fat pheasant (cock or hen) will just feed four adults. Use a brace if you have hungry teenagers, but then double all the quantities below. If you can't find Bramley apples, uses Cox's instead though add on a couple as they are smaller.

I like to prepare this dish early in the day and cook it until it is all but done, then take it out of the oven and return it again to a hot oven for the last 30-40 minutes.

It is hard to select vegetables to serve with this dish. Jacket potatoes are great but you will need two ovens as they need to cook at about 200°C/400°F/Gas Mark 6 (don't be tempted to compromise by cooking the bird and potatoes at the midway point of 180°C/350°F/Gas Mark 4 – it spoils both) and I do not like potatoes cooked in the microwave. Mashed potatoes are good perhaps cooked with celeriac, as are roast or mashed parsnips, or broccoli.

25g/1oz butter
1-2 tbsp olive oil
1 good, fat, well-hung
  pheasant

1 onion, chopped
115g/4oz piece of fat belly of
  pork, cut into 4 pieces, or
  unsmoked bacon rashers,

cut into 1cm/½in pieces
6 Bramley apples, peeled if
the skins are tough, cored
and fairly thickly sliced
150ml/5fl oz double cream
1-2 tbsp Calvados

or Cointreau
1-2 tbsp dry white wine
A little ground cinnamon
(optional)
Salt and freshly ground
black pepper

Preheat the oven to 170°C/325°F/Gas Mark 3. Heat the butter and oil in a large stainless-steel pan and brown the pheasant all over. Once the bird is browned, put it in a lidded Le Creuset casserole, put on the lid and keep warm in the oven.

Fry the onion and belly of pork lightly in the fat remaining in the pan. If needs be, add a touch more oil, but do not overdo it. Remove the onion and pork and keep warm with the pheasant. Add the apples and fry lightly until they just begin to soften, then remove and keep separately from the bird, pork and onions. Bring those back and fry briefly again in the pan and then return them to the casserole dish. Add the apples and cream to the casserole, the Calvados (or, if you have a sweet tooth, you can use Cointreau, although I prefer the apple dryness of Calvados).

I like to take up all the brown bits sticking to the bottom of the pan with 1 tbsp or so of dry white wine or water, scraping it out with a stainless-steel slice as it comes to the boil, then adding them to the casserole. If you like cinnamon, you may like to sprinkle a very little on the apples. Add some pepper and, if you wish, a little salt. Make sure the casserole lid fits tightly (if needs be put a piece of kitchen foil under it) and return it to the oven for about 2 hours, though the timing will vary with the age, size and quality of the bird. You will find that when it is almost done the legs will have begun to fall away from the body. Towards the end of the cooking time, put a serving dish in the oven to warm.

When all is done and everyone is seated at the table, put the bird on to the serving dish. If you prefer a smooth sauce, then whizz all the remaining ingredients in the casserole with a hand-held stick blender (personally I like it with a slightly lumpy texture). Either way, pour some over the bird and put the rest in a jug to pass around.

Pheasant with
red cabbage

A CLASSIC RECIPE and a good way of stretching a pheasant to provide a meal for four people, or even six with the addition of sausages to the red cabbage. Cooking pheasant is absolutely straightforward, apart, that is, from jointing the bird, which takes a bit of practice, but your butcher should do it for you – or show you how to do it. Failing that, see pages 14-16 for DIY instructions. The most important thing is to get the red cabbage right. After that, everything else falls into place.

This dish is best in December and January, when the pheasants have been stuffing themselves with food and so are really plump, and the cabbage is at its best too. It is really a complete dish served straight from the casserole. Of course, if you are feeding teenagers, then jacket potatoes would not go amiss. But if you want to impress dinner guests, Sophie Grigson, in her version of this classic recipe, suggests that you could lay it all out smartly on a big oval serving dish.

1 tbsp olive or sunflower oil
2 good, fat, well-hung
    pheasants, each jointed
    into 4 pieces
450g/1lb pork chipolata
    sausages (optional)

For the red cabbage:
1 large red cabbage, cored
    and shredded
Bramley apples (use half the
    weight of the cabbage),
    cored and sliced

Onions (use the same weight as the apples), sliced
50g/2oz raisins
3 tbsp brown sugar
1 garlic clove, finely chopped or crushed
¼-½ tsp ground cinnamon
¼-½ tsp freshly grated nutmeg
2-3 tbsp red wine vinegar
Juice of 1 orange
300ml/10 fl oz red wine
Salt and freshly ground black pepper

Preheat the oven to 150°C/300°F/Gas Mark 2. Put the shredded cabbage, apples, onions, raisins, sugar, garlic, spices and some salt and pepper in layers in a large lidded Le Creuset casserole. Put the wine vinegar, orange juice and red wine into a measuring jug and add water to make up to 600ml/1 pint. Pour over the cabbage. Put on the lid and cook for about 2 hours. Take a look after 1 hour to make sure it is not getting dry. If it is, add some more water or wine.

Once you have checked the cabbage, heat the oil in a frying pan. If you are using sausages, prick them thoroughly and then fry until they are half cooked. Remove from the pan with a slotted spoon and reserve, then brown the pheasant pieces in the fat and oil. Push the pheasant pieces and sausages well down into the cabbage. You can, if you think the juices from cooking them are not too greasy, pour them on top of the cabbage – that is just a matter of taste. Return the casserole to the oven for another 2 hours, by which time the pheasant will be thoroughly cooked.

Easiest-ever curried pheasant with dhal

CURRIES ARE OFTEN used as a way of finishing up leftover roast meat. Personally I do not think that is the best way to make a curry, or perhaps to use the leftovers, and on page 51 you will find a recipe for devilled pheasant (adapted from the usual post-Christmas devilled turkey).

If, however, you are looking at leftover pheasant, then hopefully you will have a jar of Patak's excellent korma sauce in the cupboard. There is nothing wrong with simply following the instructions on the jar, but I would lightly fry an onion and a chopped garlic clove, then add the meat, chopped into bite-size pieces, fry it all up together, keep it hot and then simply add the sauce as instructed on the label. Heat it all through, put it into a casserole and cook in the oven for 30-40 minutes at about 170°C/325°F/Gas Mark 3.

Alternatively, if you are going to curry an uncooked bird, you should follow the recipe below. If you want to keep the pheasant in large pieces, it is best to almost cook it one day, leave the meat to absorb the spices overnight and then finish cooking it the next day. In my opinion, any curry is best if it has been left to absorb all the flavours into the meat (or fish) and then reheated, otherwise it can sometimes taste like curry sauce with bits of meat (or fish) in. If you want to eat straight away, however, you will need to cut the meat into smaller pieces.

Serve the curry with plain boiled rice. There are so many 'proper' ways to cook rice that I think it simplest to follow what it says on the packet – but do buy good-quality Indian patna rice. Make sure you warm a dish in the oven shortly before you need it. Put just a little butter or oil in the bottom and if you let the rice drain well before putting it in the dish, and then turn just once to coat it with the butter, it should turn out well.

I also like to have dhal with curry, which is why I've provided a recipe for it. It is ideal if you have a hungry family. It also freezes well, so you may wish to make some extra to freeze, ready for the next curry. Add some good mango chutney and some poppadoms, naan bread or chapattis – all available at Waitrose or Sainsburys or other good stores – to make an excellent meal.

1 tbsp olive oil
    or 50g/2oz butter
1 medium onion, finely
    chopped
2 garlic cloves, finely
    chopped
1 good, fat, well-hung
    pheasant, jointed into
    4 pieces (see page 15)
1 jar at least of Patak's
    sauce, or similar

For the dahl:
225g/8oz lentils (the large
    green ones are best),

soaked in water for
    1-2 hours, or overnight
    if more convenient
½ tsp ground turmeric
½ tsp chilli powder
    (or a bit less or more
    according to taste)
1-2 tbsp olive oil
    or 25g/1oz butter
2 medium onions,
    finely chopped
227g/8oz can chopped
    tomatoes, or 3 or 4 fresh
    ones, skinned
Salt

Heat the oil or melt the butter in a frying pan and fry the onion and garlic gently until golden. Add the pheasant pieces. Stir in the curry sauce with a wooden spoon and continue frying for another 3-4 minutes or so until they are browned. Put into a casserole and cook in the oven at 170°C/325°F/Gas Mark 3 until done (1½-2 hours).

About 45 minutes before the pheasant will be ready, put the soaked lentils into about 1.2 litres/2 pints boiling water with the turmeric and chilli (and a little salt if you wish), bring to the boil and then simmer for around 30 minutes until tender. In the meantime, heat the oil or melt the butter in a frying pan and fry the onions until golden, then add the tomatoes and cook for a little longer. Add these to the cooked lentils and cook for another 5-10 minutes until the dhal is about the consistency of porridge. Serve with the pheasant.

Roast pheasant

THE PHEASANT IS a wild bird so it carries less fat than a chicken, particularly early in the season, and it needs roasting with care. Generally speaking the hen bird, though smaller, will roast better than the cock, but in any case I would rather roast pheasant in December or January than in October. It is also important to be sure that your butcher does hang the bird for at least 6-7 days (and not in a freezing-cold room!) before it is cleaned.

As always, whether roasting a chicken or game bird, the stuffing is important. Game birds need stuffings that contain fat (none of your Paxo breadcrumbs: something more like black pudding – even haggis – or fillet steak), and you will need good, fat, unsmoked bacon or sheets of pork fat to keep the bird well basted. As an alternative to using just strips of steak as a stuffing, you could try either the black pudding and oatmeal stuffing or the fruit-based stuffing opposite. (The former is a recent invention and I am still adjusting the amount of herbs to get it just right for my taste, but I include the basic recipe from which to work.)

So far as vegetables are concerned, I like this with traditional winter fare: mashed swede, shredded buttered cabbage, or perhaps roast parsnips or mashed potato with celeriac. As I think game chips (which are often served in restaurants) are a bit boring, I often serve potatoes cooked as my wife used to do, in the recipe below.

1 good, fat, well-hung
   pheasant
25g/1oz butter
50g/2oz piece of fillet steak
   (or stuffing – see below)
Fat unsmoked bacon
   or sheets of pork
   fat – enough to cover
   the pheasant

For the black pudding
stuffing:
115g/4oz black pudding
   or haggis
85g/3oz oatmeal or fresh
   white breadcrumbs
1 egg, beaten
1 small apple, chopped
1 heaped tsp chopped
   thyme
½ tsp chopped parsley
1 tsp brandy
Salt and freshly ground
   black pepper

For the fruit stuffing:
1 apple, quartered
Chopped plums or
   ready-to-eat dried
   apricots or prunes or

dates – enough to stuff
   the bird
115g/4oz fresh white
   breadcrumbs
About 25g/1oz butter

For the gravy:
1 small carrot, sliced
1 celery stick, sliced
1 small onion
   or 2 shallots, halved
1 bouquet garni
   (see page 18)
150ml/5fl oz game bird
   stock (see page 16) or
   chicken stock
A little plain flour,
   for thickening
1 glass of red wine

For the roasted sliced
potatoes:
Sufficient potatoes for
   4 people
A little oil

Preheat the oven to 200°C/400°F/Gas Mark 6. Thoroughly butter the cavity of the bird and put in the steak, cut it into strips or use one of the stuffings.

For the black pudding stuffing, mix the chopped-up black pudding, the oatmeal, the chopped apple and herbs together in a bowl, add the beaten egg, the brandy and plenty of salt and pepper. Then gently warm it all in a saucepan until it is hot before stuffing the bird. (My illustrator, Debby Mason, favours a good slug of whisky to go with the haggis to make this a 'Flying Scotsman Pheasant'.) If you would prefer the fruit stuffing, chop and mix all the ingredients thoroughly in a bowl, then warm thoroughly in a saucepan until hot, before stuffing the bird. Remember that tightly stuffing a bird with a big blob of cold stuffing will extend the cooking time by 20 minutes or even more, so it is well worth getting it hot. Cover the pheasant well with the bacon, using cocktail sticks to keep it in position.

For the gravy, put the carrot, celery, onion and bouquet garni in the bottom of a roasting tin and place a roasting rack on top. Add a little hot water, just 5mm/¼in or so, which, together with some stock, will be the base of the gravy. Place the pheasant on the rack and place in the oven. The pheasant will take 45-60 minutes (according to age and size), though a 2-year-old bird might take longer. Check to see if it is done from time to time (the juices will run clear and the legs will be falling away) and add a little more hot water if needs be to prevent the vegetables drying out.

For the sliced, roasted potatoes, scald the potatoes by bringing them to the boil in a saucepan of cold water.

Drain and then slice thinly. Place them in two layers in a lightly oiled ovenproof dish, drizzling a little oil over each layer, and put in the oven with the pheasant for the remaining half an hour of the cooking time until nicely brown, turning over if needs be to make sure they are all crisped a bit.

About 15 minutes before the pheasant will be ready, remove the bacon from the skin to crisp it. Leave the bacon in the oven so it keeps warm for serving with the bird – or if the children (or even guests) are beginning to turn nasty while waiting for food, buy them off with the crispy bacon bits.

When the pheasant is done, remove it to a dish in a warming or second oven, if you have one. If not, turn the oven off and put it on a warm serving dish, wrapped in kitchen foil and leave it to rest. Lift out the vegetable bits from the roasting tin with a slotted spoon (I think they are too good to waste and I serve them with the bird). Put the tin on the hob and add some of the stock. Turn up to the boil while scraping all the bits from the bottom of the roasting tin with a wooden spoon. Sprinkle in a shake or two of flour from a flour shaker, a little at a time, and keep at it with the spoon to work it in with no lumps. Slosh in the red wine and use as much stock as you need to make as much gravy as you like, stirring all the while with a wooden spoon until the gravy has thickened. Add the seasoning and all is ready.

Simple casseroled pheasant

THE BASIC CASSEROLED pheasant (or most other meats) is a simple enough affair. You fry some onions or shallots and pork or bacon, put them on one side, brown the bird in the oil and juices, put it all in a casserole dish, add stock and wine, then cook at 170°C/325°F/Gas Mark 3 until done (1-1½ hours). That is pretty straightforward and the art of making it into a really fine meal lies in the extras: mushrooms, apples, cabbage, cream, etc. (but not all together, needless to say). A good fat pheasant will be enough for four people, unless they are teenagers.

When serving this dish, if you are going overboard you could have croutons around it to decorate the dish. As to vegetables, I like jacket potatoes, but if you have only one oven then that is a problem as I think they need to be cooked at 200°C/400°F/Gas Mark 6 (and the microwave just makes them soggy). Mashed potato or potato and celeriac is good, mashed swede gives extra colour and I would never turn my nose up at broccoli, provided it is steaming hot and not overcooked.

1-2 tbsp olive oil
    or 50g/2oz butter
1 fat, well-hung pheasant
115g/4oz piece of fat belly
    of pork or unsmoked
    bacon, cut into 4 pieces
225g/8oz small onions
    or shallots

Glass of red or white wine
600ml/1 pint pheasant
    stock (see page 16) or
    chicken stock
1 bouquet garni
    (see page 18)
225g/8oz portabellini
    or field mushrooms

A little plain flour, for
thickening (optional)
1 tbsp redcurrant jelly

(optional)
Salt and freshly ground
black pepper

Preheat the oven to 170°C/325°F/Gas Mark 3. Heat half the oil or melt half the butter in a frying pan and brown the pheasant on all sides. Transfer it into a lidded Le Creuset casserole using a slotted spoon and keep warm in the oven. Sauté the bacon in the fat remaining in the pan and, as the fat begins to flow, add the onions and fry until golden. Use the other half of the oil or butter if needed. Return the bird to the pan, let it all warm up, then pour in the wine and let it sizzle and bubble for a moment or two, before adding the stock and bouquet garni, and seasoning with salt and pepper. Return it all to the casserole and cook in the oven for 1½-2 hours. If the lid is not tight fitting, put some kitchen foil underneath it. Watch that it does not dry out; if it looks in danger of doing so, add a little extra stock or water.

When the pheasant is almost done (that is, the legs are beginning to fall away), add the mushrooms. Of course, if you prefer, you could fry them lightly and put them in at the beginning. It is just a matter of how you like them. When everything is done, if you had to add extra liquid during cooking, you may find there is too much in the tin and the gravy looks a bit thin, in that case drain it off into a saucepan and return the casserole to the oven to keep warm, adding the plates and a serving dish too. Bring the liquid up to the boil and sprinkle in a shake or two of flour from a flour shaker while whisking or stirring with a wooden spoon until it begins to thicken. At the same time add the redcurrant jelly and it should thicken up nicely. Put the pheasant on a dish, pour the gravy over it and serve with your chosen vegetables.

Pheasant with pigs' trotters

So far as I know it was Joyce Molyneux of The Carved Angel restaurant in Dartmouth who first had the brilliant idea of using the wonderful gelatine and flavour of pigs' trotters to balance the leanness of the meat of the pheasant. Sheer culinary genius. This is my version of the trotter- and brandy-enhanced casserole. The trotters take 2 hours and should be cooked before the pheasant goes into the oven. Serve with mashed swede, mashed potato (and celeriac if you like it) or mashed or roast parsnips.

For the trotters:
2 pigs' trotters
300ml/10fl oz white wine
1 carrot, sliced
1 medium onion, sliced
1 celery stick
    or ½ fennel bulb, sliced
The usual herbs etc. A bay
    leaf, a couple of sprigs of
    thyme, garlic to taste – I
    use 3 or 4 cloves – a half
    dozen black peppercorns,
    1 bay leaf
6 black peppercorns

For the pheasant:
1 good, fat, well-hung
    pheasant
1 tbsp oil
    or 25g/1oz butter
12 shallots or really small
    onions – about the size
    of shallots
115g/4oz piece of fat belly
    of pork or unsmoked
    bacon, cut into 1cm/½in
    cubes
12 small mushrooms
1 bouquet garni (see page 18)

600ml/1 pint stock – best
   to use the stock from
   cooking the trotters (see
   above)

2 tbsp brandy
1 good large glass
   of red wine (about
   200-250ml/7-9fl oz)

Preheat the oven to 170°C/325°F/Gas Mark 3. Tidy up the trotters if your butcher did not do so. The hairs are best singed, and a pair of good kitchen scissors should remove the toenails and any other loose bits. Put everything into a lidded Le Creuset casserole with 300ml/10fl oz water and bring to the boil. This usually brings up a scum, which is best removed. Then put on the lid and cook in the oven for about 2 hours or until it is tender, keeping an eye on it to make sure it does not dry out. Add more hot water if needs be.

To cook the pheasant, heat the oil or melt the butter in a stainless-steel frying pan and brown the pheasant all over. Remove with a slotted spoon and keep warm in a large Pyrex (or similar) dish in the oven with the cooked trotters. Brown the shallots and the pork cubes in the frying pan until the shallots turn soft and golden. Return the pheasant to the pan and, when all is nicely hot, pour in 1½ tbsp of the brandy. Warm the remainder in the spoon using a match, and when all the fumes are rising nicely, light it and pour that in too. When the flames have subsided, return the pheasant, onions and pork to the Pyrex dish. Remove the trotters from the oven and add them to the pheasant dish. Strain the stock and pour it into the pan. Add the red wine, scraping up all the tasty bits stuck on the bottom of the pan, and bring it all to the boil.

Now get everything – the bird, the trotters and the sauce – back into the casserole, adding the mushrooms and bouquet garni. If you like (and my wife does), you can also add the vegetables used with the trotters to make the stock. Put the lid on and cook in the oven for 1½ hours – or more if the pheasant needs it. When the pheasant is ready, put it and the trotters on to a warm dish, surrounded by the shallots and mushrooms, and serve.

Pheasant with brown rice

THIS IS ONE OF the best complete meals, which can be prepared, put in the oven, washing up done and almost forgotten until it comes out to the table. It is based on those chicken dishes you find from Greece and Spain and, as ever, you can adjust the ingredients to suit yourself. But do stick quite rigidly to the quantities of rice and liquids. I tend to measure rice by volume rather than weight and you will need twice the volume of liquid (stock and white wine) as of rice.

I prefer to do the frying bit of this recipe in my favourite deep, double-handled, stainless-steel frying pan, and then transfer everything to a brown pottery casserole pot that looks good on the table and holds heat better than steel, although I sometimes put the steel pan into the oven if I am in a hurry. Alternatively, you can do everything in a lidded Le Creuset casserole. If you have a gas hob you may prefer to let it all simmer there rather than use the oven, but I think electric plates (however good) are not suitable for long simmering.

1 good, fat, well-hung pheasant, jointed into 4 pieces (see page 15)
3 tbsp olive oil
1 Spanish onion or 2 regular ones, thickly sliced
2 red peppers or Romano peppers, deseeded, halved and cut into 1cm/½in wide strips

2 tomatoes, chopped (or use sundried tomatoes in oil)
Garlic, to taste. I use at least two cloves crushed or chopped
250ml/8fl oz brown rice (preferably basmati, which cooks more quickly)

250ml/8fl oz game bird
   stock (see page 16)
   or chicken stock
250ml/8fl oz dry white wine
2 tbsp tomato purée

1 tsp thyme, chopped
1 tsp chopped tarragon
½ tsp chopped rosemary
Salt and freshly ground
   black pepper

If you want a real Spanish flavour, you can add some halved black olives, a sliced orange, and some slices of Spanish chorizo sausage, about 115g/4oz – but don't forget to skin them.

Preheat the oven to 180°C/350°F/Gas Mark 4. Heat the oil in a large frying pan and fry the pheasant pieces briefly – just until a gentle brown on both sides – then pop them into the casserole, put the lid on and keep warm in the oven. Next, fry the onion and peppers, and when they begin to look cooked (4-5 minutes), add the garlic (and chorizo if you are using it). Stir in the rice with a wooden spoon to take up the remaining oil, just as you would for a risotto, then pour in the liquid – wine or stock – add the tomato purée and tomatoes and season with salt and pepper. Bring it all just to the boil, then simmer for a few minutes.

Now remove the pheasant from the casserole on to a plate or dish. Put the rice mixture and liquid into the casserole, then put the pheasant on top, add the herbs and put the lid on. (If you are going for a really Iberian style, add the olives and orange pieces on top.) Cook in the oven for about 1 hour, but check after 45 minutes to make sure it is not drying out. If it is, add some water or wine. The cooking time is really more dependent on the rice than the pheasant: it needs to be soft but not mushy.

Pheasant breasts with beetroot, potato and parsnip

YOU MAY HAVE bought the pheasant breasts on their own, or used the legs grilled, devilled or as a starter or snack. At any rate, for this recipe you will need two breasts each or three for larger appetites.

I think beetroot is a much abused and underrated vegetable that in my childhood was always served swimming in vinegar to accompany cold meat and salad, or to eke out the cheese ration in sandwiches. Eaten young, just simply boiled or as one of a tray of mixed roast vegetables, they are terrific – and they add colour to a dish that would otherwise look a bit pallid. Just remember to break off rather than cut the leaves, leave on the root during cooking and do not cut the beetroot in any way or it will bleed and lose colour. This recipe serves 2-3 people.

6 pheasant breasts
50g/2oz butter
2 tsp olive oil
2 or 3 small (but not button-sized) beetroot, leaves broken off and root intact
680g/1½lb potatoes (King Edward or Maris Piper), cut into chunks

225g/8oz parsnips, cut into chunks
1 good-sized Bramley apple, peeled, cored and cut into chunks
1 tbsp double cream or crème fraîche
Lots of chopped parsley or snipped chives – 1½ tbsp in all

1 glass white wine
185ml/6fl oz game bird
    stock (see page 16) or
    chicken stock

2 tsp plain flour salt
Mixed root vegetable crisps,
    to serve (optional)

It is best to start with the vegetables. The beetroot
needs cooking for around 60 minutes or more. Bring it to
the boil, then cover and simmer until tender. Meanwhile,
boil the potatoes and parsnips separately until tender
(15-20 minutes). They will benefit from a pinch – but
only a pinch – of salt. Soften the apple by popping it in
with the parsnips or potatoes for a few minutes at the end
of the cooking time.

Preheat the oven to a low setting for keeping plates,
food etc. warm. Once the potatoes and parsnips are
cooked and the apple softened, drain them all, mix them
in one saucepan and let them dry off over a low heat.
Then mash as you would plain potatoes with half of the
butter, plus the cream and the parsley or chives. Put in a
lidded serving dish and keep warm in the oven or over a
low heat – but do not let it dry out. Drain the beetroot
and cut into thick slices, then put them in the warm
oven too.

Now turn to the pheasant. Fry the breasts in a good
steel pan in the olive oil until brown on both sides – it
should take only a couple of minutes. Pour in the wine,
bring briefly to the boil and reduce by about a half. Add
the stock and turn down to a brisk simmer until the
breasts are cooked. (If they have come from a good young
bird, that should be about 5 minutes.) While that is going
on, mix the remaining butter with the flour to make a

beurre manié (see page 18) and keep on one side. When the breasts are done, transfer them to a dish and keep warm in the oven with the vegetables.

Now raise the heat under the frying pan containing the meat juices and stock and, little bit by little bit, add the beurre manié, stirring with a wooden spoon as you do so, until it thickens and comes to the boil. That is it. Bring out the dish with the mashed potato and parsnips and arrange the pheasant breasts and beetroot slices on top, add the sauce and it is ready to serve. For a bit of extra show, it is quite nice to decorate around the dish with some of those rather good mixed root vegetable crisps you find in the better places – like my village shop, Waitrose and other good supermarkets.

Pheasant breasts with crème fraîche

THIS IS A SIMPLE fried breast recipe. One breast per person may be enough for light eaters, but those with better appetites would need both breasts of the average hen bird. Alternatively you could serve a leg and a breast for each person.

The amount of paprika is not a misprint – I do mean 1 tablespoon. The caraway seeds are not absolutely essential but they do add something to the sauce, so worth trying. Serve this dish with your favourite potatoes and vegetables. Serves 2.

2 tbsp olive oil
  or 50g/2oz butter
2 pheasant breasts and 2 legs
Roughly 300ml/10fl oz

crème fraîche
1 tbsp paprika
1 tbsp caraway seeds
Chopped parsley, to garnish

Fry the pheasant pieces gently in the oil or butter in a good heavy steel frying pan. The breasts will need about 5 minutes a side – the legs (if you are using them) more like 7½-8 minutes, so start them first. When they are done, add the crème fraîche, then stir in the paprika with a wooden spoon and let the mixture simmer gently – do not let it boil or it will separate – for about 7-10 minutes. At the end add the caraway seeds, garnish with parsley and serve. It really could hardly be simpler.

Devilled pheasant (or partridge)

WE STARTED BY devilling the leftover turkey many, many years ago, then found a recipe for devilling the brown meat separately and serving it with the white meat in a cream sauce in Jane Grigson's great 1979 book *English Food*. It has changed a bit over the years in our kitchen, but not too much for the worse I hope. Here it has been adapted for pheasant or partridge, which is especially useful if, towards the end of the season, the children are starting to say 'not pheasant again'.

These quantities are enough for a light supper dish. We like this with one (or two) chilled or frozen ready-to-cook garlic-butter baguettes, available, of course, from all good supermarkets. Remember they take about 20 minutes to cook.

1 cold roast or simply
   casseroled pheasant
   (or 2 partridges)
2 tsp chopped parsley
2 tsp chopped basil

For the devil sauce:
2 tbsp mango chutney
   (preferably Green Label)
1 tbsp Worcestershire sauce
1 tbsp Dijon mustard

2 tsp dry mustard powder
¼ tsp cayenne pepper
1 tbsp olive oil
25g/1oz butter

For the cream sauce:
175g/6oz butter
200ml/7fl oz double
   or thick single cream
Juice of ½ lemon
Salt and ground black pepper

Dismember the bird(s), cutting the brown meat off the legs, thighs and wings, and cutting off and shredding the breast meat. Keep separate and put aside in the fridge.

Put the devil sauce ingredients into a bowl and mix thoroughly, making sure the lumpy bits of the chutney are mulched well into the mixture. Immerse the brown meat in the sauce and let it marinate in it for 3 or 4 hours in the fridge if you can.

When you are ready to cook, line the grill pan with kitchen foil, distribute the brown meat with as much sauce on it as you can onto the rack and put under a really hot grill to brown and just beginning to crisp. Meanwhile, make the cream sauce. Melt the butter in a large stainless-steel pan, add the cream, let it come almost to the boil while you keep stirring it with a wooden spoon to help it to thicken, then add the white meat and make sure it is all hot. Add the lemon juice, salt and pepper. Meanwhile heat a serving dish and plates. Now put the devilled meat at one end of the serving dish and the white at the other, sprinkled with the herbs to give a nice brown, white and green colour to it all.

Highland pheasant

NOT ONLY ARE Scottish grouse rightly famed for their quality but the pheasants from up there are pretty good too. This recipe gives a Scottish flavour to even a Sussex bird and makes an enjoyable light supper or luncheon dish. You might serve the patties with bashed tatties and neeps all garnished with a sprig of heather – or Sassenachs might prefer potatoes and celeriac mash. DM.

4 pheasant breasts
1 haggis
175g/6oz ready-to-eat dried apricots, finely chopped
3 tbsp whisky
12 dry-cured streaky bacon rashers

Olive oil for drizzling
125ml/4fl oz game bird stock (see page 16) or chicken stock
2 tsp cornflour
125ml/4fl oz double cream
1 tbsp chopped parsley

Preheat the oven to 180°C/350°F/Gas Mark 4. The easiest way to flatten the pheasant breasts is to put them between sheets of cling film on a wooden board and bash them with a wooden rolling pin.

Crumble the haggis into a bowl, mix in the chopped apricots and pour 1 tbsp of the whisky over it. Let it infuse for a few minutes. Divide the divine mixture into four portions and press into patties. Fold the pheasant breasts around these patties, wrap each one with three rashers of bacon. Cocktail sticks may be useful to keep them together. Put them on a baking tray (preferably non-stick), drizzle with oil and cook for 45-55 minutes.

While the haggis-pheasant patties are cooking, you should prepare the sauce. Heat the stock gently while stirring in the cornflour with a wooden spoon, a bit at a time to avoid any lumps. Add the remaining whisky, then let it all simmer for about 5 minutes. Pour in the cream gradually and let it all warm through. Add the chopped parsley and spoon the sauce over the patties as they come out of the oven and are on a serving dish.

Pheasant pâté

THIS RECIPE IS one from Game To Eat – the organisation founded by The Countryside Alliance to promote the eating of game. I found it very straightforward.

350g/12oz minced pheas-
  ant and 1 pheasant
  breast, diced
225g/8oz dry-cured streaky
  bacon rashers
675g/1½lb fat belly of pork
2 tbsp brandy
1 garlic clove, crushed

6-8 juniper berries,
  chopped
2 tbsp chopped rosemary
2 tbsp chopped thyme
Small bunch of coriander,
  chopped
A few bay leaves, for
  decoration

Chop half the bacon into small (5-10mm/¼-½in) squares and mix in a bowl with the rest of the ingredients (except the other half of the bacon rashers). Leave for an hour or so to mix the flavours thoroughly.

Preheat the oven to 150°C/300°F/Gas Mark 2. Put the ingredients into a Le Creuset terrine dish and smooth the top. (If you have not got this dish, use an ovenproof baking dish of roughly the same dimensions but go out tomorrow and buy one.) Lay the remaining streaky rashers diagonally over the top. Decorate with the bay leaves and then put the dish into a roasting tin of hot water to come halfway up the sides and cook for 2-2½ hours with the lid on the terrine or a cover of extra thick (or doubled) kitchen foil over the top. You will know it is cooked when the pâté has shrunk away from the sides of the tin and when the juices run clear if you stick in a skewer.

When it is done, remove from the oven and squeeze the pâté down with a similar-sized dish or even a piece of flat, smooth wood with something heavy (packets of sugar, tins of something – or use a house brick wrapped in kitchen foil). When it is cool, put it in the fridge for a few hours – or overnight – before shaking the pâté out ready to serve.

Pheasant Bobotie bake

I FIRST CAME across Bobotie at John Tovey's wonderful Miller Howe restaurant in the Lake District.

I love the combination of game, fruit and spices, so thought pheasant rather than lamb or beef would be an interesting change. You will need some biryani spices, which are very easy to prepare and will make the kitchen smell wonderful! The remaining mixture will keep in an airtight jar and is a great rub for lamb chops. DM.

Biryani spices:
1 cinnamon stick
2 tsp fennel seeds
1 tsp cumin seeds
2 bay leaves
5 cardamom pods

6 cloves
3 tbsp coriander seeds
1 star anise
1 tsp black peppercorns
2 tsp mace
4-5 tsp chilli powder

Apart from the mace and chilli powder, dry roast gently all the above ingredients until toasted. Then add the mace and chilli. Allow to cool then grind to a fine powder in a blender or a pestle and mortar.

675g/1½lb pheasant, minced
2 slices white bread, crusts removed and torn into small pieces
125ml/4fl oz milk

2 large onions, peeled and chopped
2 tbsp biryani spice mix
4 tsp medium curry powder
2 large tomatoes, peeled and chopped

2 apples, peeled and chopped
1 tbsp lemon zest
½ tsp sugar
75g/3oz sultanas
2 tsp salt
2 tbsp apricot jam
10 dried ready-to-eat
    apricots, chopped
1 egg
200ml/7fl oz milk

Small handful of flaked
    almonds
Vegetable oil, for frying

For the topping:
675g/1½lb potatoes (or half
    and half sweet potatoes)
2 eggs
250ml/9fl oz milk
1 tsp turmeric

Preheat the oven to 170°C/325°F/Gas Mark 3. In a small bowl, pour the milk over the torn-up bread and leave to soak. For the topping peel the potatoes and boil in lightly salted water until just cooked. Drain and set aside.

Heat 3 tbsp of oil in a heavy-based pan and cook the onions until soft and golden. Add the biryani spices and curry powder and fry for a few more minutes. Add a little more oil if necessary.

Now add the tomatoes, apples, lemon zest, sugar, and sultanas, mix well and fry for a further minute. Add the minced meat, stirring well to break it up and combine it with the spices and onions. Stir in the salt.

Mix in the apricot jam and dried apricots. The meat should be gently coloured, but not completely cooked. Leave it to cool for a few minutes then add the soggy bread and milk mixture. You may need to break up the bread a little more. Whisk the egg and 200ml of milk and stir into the meat.

Grease an oven dish, and pour in the meat mixture. Scatter with the flaked almonds. Place in the preheated oven.

While it is cooking, dice the cooled potatoes.

Remove the dish after 40 minutes and top the meat and almonds with the potatoes.

Beat the egg, milk and turmeric to make a lovely yellow custard and pour over the potatoes.

Return to oven and bake until the egg custard has set, about 15 minutes.

Serve with a crispy salad.

Festive pheasant pie

THIS WAS INSPIRED by my memories as a small child beating for my grandfather's shoot on the Blackdown Hills in Somerset at Christmas. The grandchildren would be piled into the back of his Land Rover and rattled and bounced over the fields. Lunch was always lukewarm tomato soup from battered old Thermos flasks. We would always return home with a brace of pheasants and my mother would hang them in the larder. I'd always forget they were there and would be startled each time I opened the door.

I make my own cranberry sauce, but you could use a jar of ready-made sauce. Just depends how sweet you like it. I like to add a good slosh of port to it. DM.
Serves 6-8.

For the pastry:
75g/3oz each of butter
    and lard
350g/12oz plain flour
Cold water

For the cranberry sauce:
300g/10oz cranberries
1 orange, zest and juice
1 lemon, zest and juice
150g/5oz sugar (or to taste)
175ml/6fl oz lemon and
    orange juice (from

orange and lemon
    above), if not enough,
    make up with water
4 tbsp port

For the filling:
675g/1½lb pheasant,
    cut into smallish pieces
1 tsp mace
5 eggs
450g/1lb sausagemeat
2 tsp fresh thyme
1 tsp fresh sage, chopped

12 spring onions, finely sliced,
    white and green parts
½ lemon, zest and juice

250ml/9fl oz double cream
Salt and freshly ground
    black pepper

Start by making the pastry. You could use ready-made shortcrust. Cut the butter and lard into cubes and rub into the flour until it resembles fine breadcrumbs. Pour in some cold water, a spoonful at a time to bring the mix together and form into a doughy ball. Put it into a bowl, cover and pop in the fridge.

To make the cranberry sauce, rinse the cranberries discarding any that look wrinkly and squishy. Place in a heavy-based saucepan and add some of the sugar, water, the lemon and orange zest and juice. Simmer gently stirring occasionally until the cranberries have split, released their juices and are soft. Taste for level of sweetness required, adding more sugar if necessary. Finally, stir in the port and leave to cool.

Hard boil 4 of the eggs. Place eggs in a saucepan of cold water, bring to the boil, cover and turn off the heat. Leave for 8-9 minutes for a firm but still soft-centred egg. Cool and peel.

Combine the pheasant meat with the mace and season with salt and freshly ground black pepper.

In a separate bowl, mix the sausagemeat with the chopped herbs, spring onions (you could use a little red onion instead), lemon juice and zest. When well mixed, add the double cream – you want it to have the consistency of a sponge cake mixture so it can easily form layers and is not too dense when cooked.

Preheat the oven to 200°C/400°F/Gas Mark 6.

Using a 22cm/9in loose-bottomed cake tin, line the bottom and sides with just over two thirds of the pastry.

Spread about half the sausagemeat evenly over the pastry base, then about half of the cranberry sauce. Next, layer half of the pheasant pieces. Cover with the remaining sausagemeat and the rest of the pheasant. Nestle the four whole hard-boiled eggs into the pheasant layer and top with the remaining cranberry sauce.

Beat the remaining egg and brush edges of pastry case. Roll out the remaining pastry and cover the pie. Seal and crimp the edges. If there is any remaining pastry left from trimming the top, cut into shapes to decorate the top of the pie. I cut leaves or use an Easter chick-shaped cutter. Finally, brush with the rest of the beaten egg.

Cook in the centre of the oven for 30 minutes, then reduce the temperature to 180°C/350°F/Gas Mark 4 for an hour. Leave to cool before cutting.

Pheasant Scotch eggs

I'M A BIG FAN of Scotch eggs, great for picnics and you can vary the flavours by adding herbs and spices to the sausagemeat and breadcrumbs. These are baked in the oven so easier and healthier than deep-fat frying. DM. Makes 4.

275g/10oz pheasant (finely chopped, I use the leg meat as it's a fiddle to extract and the pieces are quite small)
5 eggs
50g/2oz sausagemeat (add some finely chopped sage and some red onion if you like)
50g/2oz apricots (the ready-to-eat ones, finely chopped)
115g/4oz breadcrumbs
Flour to dust
Salt and freshly ground black pepper

Hard boil 4 of the eggs. Place eggs in a saucepan of cold water, bring to the boil, cover and turn off the heat. Leave for 8-9 minutes for a firm but still soft-centred egg. Leave to cool in very cold water.

Preheat the oven to 190°C/375°F/Gas Mark 5.

Mix the chopped pheasant, sausagemeat and apricots together, adding seasoning and a little flour if too sticky. Divide mixture into 4 pieces.

Peel the hard-boiled eggs. Using your hands and some more flour, gently flatten each piece of meat mixture and wrap around each egg. Carefully roll it around in your hands to seal any joins otherwise the meat may split apart whilst cooking.

Beat the remaining egg to coat the meaty balls then roll them in the breadcrumbs.

Place on non-stick baking parchment on a baking tray for about 35 minutes until lightly browned.

Delicious straight from the oven or cold with chutney.

Scrumptious scrumpy pheasant

THIS IS A SLIGHTLY rustic version without Calvados and cream of *Faisan Normande* or as I like to think of it Norman's Pheasant. Born and brought up in the West Country, I thought some of our excellent cider and a mixture of apples and pears would be a good alternative. DM. Serves 2.

1 whole pheasant, oven ready
1 large Bramley apple, peeled,
    cored and sliced
2 Granny Smiths, peeled,
    cored and sliced
1 pear, peeled, cored and sliced

50g/2oz butter
250ml/9fl oz dry cider
Pinch of cinnamon
1 star anise
Salt and freshly ground
    black pepper

Preheat the oven to 190°C/375°F /Gas Mark 5. Using a third of the butter, gently colour the apple and pear slices over a fast heat.

Remove from the pan, set aside and sprinkle with a little salt and pepper.

Heat the rest of the butter and sauté the pheasant until golden brown, 3-5 minutes on its side, turn onto its breast and cook for another 2-3 minutes.

Spread the apple and pear mixture into the bottom of an ovenproof dish. Place the pheasant on top, pour over the cider, add a pinch of cinnamon, the star anise and season with salt and pepper.

Cook, uncovered for 30 minutes. Set aside, covered to rest for about five minutes. Serve straight from the dish with the apple, pear and cider sauce. Creamy mashed potato and broccoli is a good accompaniment, as well as the remains of the bottle of cider.

One pot pheasant and coconut curry

THIS VERY QUICK curry has a couple of optional ingredients – worth adding if you can find them, tamarind which has a lovely fresh tangy flavour and Nigella seeds which taste slightly bitter but have a wonderful black peppery, oregano-like taste. DM.

4 pheasant breasts, cut into bite-size chunks
1 medium onion, thinly sliced
1 green pepper, seeded and thickly sliced
1 garlic clove, finely chopped
1 red or green chilli, seeded and thinly sliced
5cm/2in piece ginger, finely chopped
2 tbsp tomato purée
1 tsp ground turmeric
2 tsp mustard seeds

400ml tin coconut milk (light or full fat)
2 tbsp tamarind pulp soaked for half an hour in a little hot water then pressed through a sieve to remove any fibre
1 tbsp light soy sauce
1 tsp Nigella seeds
Generous handful fresh coriander, chopped
Squeeze of lime juice
Olive oil, for frying

In a large wok, frying pan or casserole dish heat a couple of tablespoons of olive oil. Add the onion and green pepper stirring occasionally until softened and starting to colour. Then add the garlic, chilli and ginger and continue cooking for a couple of minutes. Keep an eye on the heat and if necessary add a little more olive oil if the mixture looks like sticking, then stir in the tomato purée, turmeric and mustard seeds.

Add the chopped pheasant breasts and stir until the meat is well sealed and has browned. Give the tin of coconut milk a good shake and add with the tamarind paste to the pan.

Simmer gently and cook for five minutes or so until the pheasant is cooked.

Finally, stir in the soy sauce and Nigella seeds, add a good squeeze of lime, sprinkle with the fresh coriander and serve with basmati rice or some naan bread.

Curried pheasant and pigeon with rice

THIS IS A POST-Christmas recipe for using up the last of the season's pheasants.

1 pheasant
4 pigeon breasts
2 cloves garlic
½ tsp peppercorns
1 x 290g jar Patek's Korma
    Spice Paste
½ onion, chopped
400g tin chopped tomatoes
2 tbsp olive oil

For the stock:
1 tsp cumin
1 tsp cinnamon

Salt and pepper

For the garnish:
3-4 almonds, chopped
2 tbsp dessicated coconut
2 tbsp sultanas
Rice. This is a matter of
    choice. I like either
    Waitrose's white or brown
    basmati rice and usually I
    use rather less than
    suggested on the packet,
    except for teenagers

Start by cleaning, removing excess fat from the pheasant (of which there is often plenty by the end of the season), then de-boning the bird.

Cut the pheasant meat and pigeon breasts into bite-sized pieces. Put the bones, skin, salt and pepper, cumin and cinnamon into a saucepan with 1.2 litres/2 pints of water. Bring up to the boil, then reduce the heat to simmer for half an hour. Once it is cool, skim off any excess fat.

Preheat the oven to 180°C/350°F/Gas Mark 4. Put the meat, garlic, peppercorns, curry paste, chopped onion, chopped tomatoes and two tablespoons of olive oil into a good heavy-lidded casserole dish and cook in the oven for 1½ hours.

That should give time for a cup of tea before tackling the rice. Wash the rice well with cold water in a sieve. Then follow the instructions on the pack of your choice. Usually that is to cook with twice the volume of water, bringing it to the boil then turning it down to simmer for about 20 or 30 minutes. For this recipe use the stock rather than water.

Then turn again to that meat. Bring the casserole out of the oven, spread the rice evenly over the meat and scatter the almonds, coconut and sultanas over that.

Put a piece of cooking foil over the casserole dish and replace the lid on top of that and return to the oven turned down to 150°C/300°F/Gas Mark 2 for ten or fifteen minutes. That will give the cook time for a glass of cool dry white wine and to make sure that the others are seated before bringing the casserole to the table.

Moroccan roast pheasant with couscous and chicory

ANOTHER SPICY DISH – very easy to prepare, full of flavour and goes wonderfully with chicory and couscous. DM. Serves 2.

1 pheasant, whole and
    oven ready
115g/4oz butter
1 tbsp Ras el hanout
1 tsp ground ginger
1 tsp cinnamon
1 tsp turmeric
½ preserved lemon
2 banana shallots, halved
    lengthways and finely
    sliced
175g/6oz couscous

2 chicory heads, bases
    trimmed, tatty leaves
    removed and cut in half
    lengthways
1 tsp caster sugar
Squeeze lemon juice
Salt and freshly ground
    black pepper
Knob of butter for couscous
    and chicory
Olive oil, for frying

Preheat the oven to 200°C/400°F/Gas Mark 6. Heat a splash of olive oil and fry the pheasant on all sides until it is a lovely nutty brown. Remove from the pan.

Soften the butter and thoroughly mix in the spices. Place the preserved lemon in the cavity of the pheasant and rest on top of the shallots in a roasting tin. Spread the spiced butter all over the pheasant, it will melt a little on the warm bird.

Put it uncovered in the oven. It should take about 30 minutes unless it is a particularly plump bird, in which case give it 5-10 minutes longer. If you can pull the leg away from the body easily with no evidence of pink or red flesh, it's ready.

Cover with kitchen foil and a clean tea towel and allow to rest for 5 minutes.

For the chicory, heat a little olive oil and a knob of butter and fry the chicory carefully on each side for about 3 minutes until golden brown. Add a splash of water to steam it slightly. Sprinkle with the sugar then turn the chicory over and cook for another couple of minutes. Squeeze over a little lemon juice and a grind of black pepper. Fry for a minute or two longer until it is caramelised and the leaves are tender.

Pour a cup of boiling stock or lightly salted water onto the couscous, cover and leave for 5 minutes. Fluff it up with a fork and it's ready to serve – you can add some dried fruit, spices or a little butter if you like.

Carve the pheasant and serve on a bed of couscous with the buttery shallots, juices and the chicory.

Cajun pheasant wraps

A QUICK AND EASY light supper or picnic dish. Cajun
spice mix can be bought ready-made or easily mixed at
home and it will keep in an airtight jar. DM.
Makes 8.

450g/1lb pheasant breast or
    leg cut into 1cm/½in wide
    strips
1 shallot, cut in half length-
    wise and sliced thinly
300ml /10fl oz sour cream
2 tsp Cajun spice mix
Zest and juice of 1 lime

For the Cajun spice mix:
(combine all the below and
keep in an airtight jar):
1 tsp salt
1 tsp freshly ground
    black pepper
1 tsp cayenne pepper

1 tsp dried oregano
1 tsp dried thyme
2 tsp sweet paprika

To serve:
½ cucumber, seeded and
    finely diced
3 tomatoes, seeded and
    finely chopped
Fresh coriander, chopped
2 avocados
Soft tortilla wraps
Salad leaves
Chilli sauce
Black pepper

Place the sliced shallot into a shallow baking tray. In a
bowl stir the pheasant pieces into half the sour cream, the
Cajun spices and the zest of the lime. Season with salt and
mix thoroughly to make sure the pheasant is well coated.
Spread the pheasant mixture evenly over the bed of shallot.

Place the pheasant under a preheated grill, set to its highest setting and grill for 12-15 minutes, keep an eye on it and turn it halfway through to ensure it is evenly cooked.

Mix up the cucumber, tomatoes and coriander. Mash up the avocados to make a guacamole with the juice of the lime and a dash of chilli sauce and some black pepper.

Wrap the meat in the tortillas with the salad, tomato mix, the guacamole and a good dollop of the remaining sour cream.

'Despite quite colourful plumage they are remarkably difficult to spot on the ground. They fly low and because they are smaller than pheasants they look to be (but are not) a lot faster'

Partridge

Phasianidae family

Partridge, 78

Partridge with pears and
blue cheese, 80

Roast partridge, 83

Partridge hot pot, 86

Partridge with dhal, 88

Partridge risotto, 90

Partridge paella, 92

Partridge tagine with olives
and lemon, 94

Partridge

THE ENGLISH OR Grey Partridge *(Perdix perdix)*, although widespread in England, much of Wales, southern and eastern Scotland and Ireland, has had a hard time during the last century. It lost nesting sites as hedges were removed to increase field sizes, and the use of pesticides robbed partridge chicks of the aphids and weevils that are essential in their first weeks of life before they become largely vegetarian as adult birds. Even then, herbicides deprive them of chickweed and other food plants.

The introduction of the Red-legged Partridge *(Alectoris rufa)* or the French partridge of the 18th century did not help our native species. It is now established over most of England and parts of eastern Scotland. Once they are plucked I cannot tell the difference, but most partridges in the butcher's shop are Red-legged, which are slightly larger and, at just over 450g/1lb, weigh a little heavier than the English or Grey bird.

Partridges do not like wet heavy clay land and are most at home amongst the smaller fields and cereal crops of places like the South Downs, or heaths and dry arable land. The Red-legged Partridges are really Iberian birds and the dry stony uplands of central Spain are home to some of the best partridges I have ever seen. Despite having quite colourful plumage, they are remarkably difficult to spot on the ground. They fly low and, because they are smaller than pheasants, they look to be (but are not) a lot faster.

You should find partridges in the shops, ready to cook for about £3 to £4. Like pheasants, they need to have been hung for 6-7 days. A single bird is plenty enough for one person or would stretch to a light meal for two. Partridges casserole well and are easier and quicker to roast than a pheasant, and have a more delicate flavour. So much so that one's first thought is often simply to roast them. However, partridge hot pots or casseroles – particularly with lentils and/or cabbage – will certainly reward the extra time and trouble in preparation.

Partridge with pears and blue cheese

THIS IS MY VERSION of a recipe suggested by Game To Eat, a campaign that exists to promote the game meat industry. The recipe rests on the sound idea that since both partridges and cheese go well with pears, it's a good idea to put them together.

As to vegetables, you cannot go wrong with either those baby new potatoes or crispy jacket ones and whatever vegetables look good in the shops. Parsnips, mashed or, if you had room in the cooker, roasted and broad beans or runners are ideal. You might also like to serve sliced roasted potatoes (see pages 37-39), which are better than game chips.

Partridges. 1 per person
50g/2oz butter softened
2 streaky bacon rashers
    per bird
Pears, 1 per bird if small
    (such as Rocha) or ½ pear
    per bird if large (such as
    Conference)

The remaining ingredients
are sufficient for 4 birds:
Vegetables for gravy –
    small onions or shallots,
    a carrot, stick of celery
1 glass of red wine
Chicken stock cube
    (optional)
A little plain flour, for
    thickening
115g/4oz blue cheese, cut
    thinly into shavings

Preheat the oven to 200°C/400°F/Gas Mark 6. Tidy up the birds, trimming off the ends of the wings and plucking off any feathers. Rub a little of the butter around the insides and outsides of the birds and cover the legs and breasts with the bacon (use cocktail sticks to keep in place). Stuff the birds with a piece of pear – probably about a quarter will be enough.

Put the onions, carrot and celery pieces in the bottom of a roasting tin with about 150ml/5fl oz boiling water – but make sure there is enough to cover the floor of the tin (the water needs to be boiling or it will take ages to get hot in the oven). Put a roasting rack in the tin and place the birds on the rack. Cover the whole lot with kitchen foil and put into the oven for 30 minutes. (Yes, it is longer than for simple roast partridge, but the temperature is lower and they are under foil.)

While the birds are cooking, slice the rest of the pears in roundels or wagon wheels and remove the cores. Melt the rest of the butter in an oven dish. Turn the slices of pear in the melted butter and put them into the oven with the birds for the last 10 minutes of their cooking time.

After 30 minutes, remove the foil round the birds to let them and the bacon crisp for a further 10 minutes. The smart way to do this is to put the birds on their rack in another tin and return to the oven. You can then take the first tin, remove the vegetables (if you like, save them in the warming oven with the plates). Bring the juices in the pan to the boil over a hot plate or gas ring, add a glass of red wine and thicken with flour (and a stock cube if you like). Use a wooden spoon to scrape all the bits off the bottom and if you get it right this will also clean the pan!

Cooking times vary with the birds, your oven and to your taste. Serve the partridges and the bacon (if crisp enough, broken up) with the thickened sauce and the pears with the blue cheese shavings on top alongside them.

Roast partridge

THIS REALLY COULD not be easier. It is best to keep it simple and I would serve the roast bird and roast potatoes with broccoli (but that is because I like roast potatoes and broccoli) and I would not bother with bread sauce (because I think it is boring) but I give a recipe for it anyway.

According to the size of the potatoes you will probably need to start them cooking in the roasting tin before the birds go in on the rack over them. However, small new potatoes seem to be available throughout the winter these days and they are ideal as they take only about 20 minutes and so can go in at the same time as the birds.

As ever, timing is the tricky thing in cooking, but if you make sure the gravy and bread sauce are done a little ahead of the birds, and that the broccoli is finishing cooking as the birds come out of the oven (cold broccoli is awful), all will be well.

4 partridges, wings clipped off and reserved for the stock
Knob of butter, softened
2 large pears (such as Conference), halved, or 4 small pears (such as Rocha)
2 streaky bacon rashers or 8 back bacon rashers

Potatoes, for roasting

For the gravy:
Partridge wings and giblets (if you have them)
1 small onion, sliced
1 carrot, chopped
1 celery stick, chopped
1 bay leaf

Thyme, parsley, oregano or whatever, but not anything as strong as rosemary
Little plain flour, for thickening
Chicken stock cube (optional)
1 heaped tsp redcurrant jelly (optional)
1 glass of red wine
Salt and freshly ground black pepper

For the bread sauce:
115g/4oz day-old white bread, thickly sliced then broken into bits
300ml/10fl oz milk
1 small onion, halved
3 black peppercorns
2 cloves (if you like them)
1 bay leaf
15g/½oz butter
Salt and freshly ground black pepper

To make the stock for the gravy, put the wings, giblets (if you have them), onion, carrot, celery, herbs, wine and about 300ml/10fl oz water into a saucepan. Bring to the boil, then reduce to a simmer for half an hour.

Meanwhile, put all the ingredients for the bread sauce, except for the butter, in a pan and leave to soak for about half an hour.

While the stock is simmering and the bread sauce ingredients are soaking, rub the butter over the birds inside and out. Stuff each bird with a whole or half pear, depending on size. Cover with the bacon rashers, using cocktail sticks to keep in place.

Preheat the oven to 230°C/450°F/Gas Mark 8. Put the new potatoes in the bottom of a roasting tin and put a roasting rack on top. Cook in the oven for 10 minutes, then place the birds on the rack and cook for a further 20 minutes. While the birds are cooking, warm the bread sauce ingredients, add the butter and let it all thicken over a very low heat, stirring occasionally with a wooden spoon, for about 15 minutes. Season to give it some taste. Take out the onion, bay leaf, peppercorns and cloves and put in a dish in the warm oven.

Meanwhile, sieve the stock into a pan and bring to the bubble, then thicken by sprinkling a shake or two of flour from a flour shaker and stirring with a wooden spoon. Season with salt and pepper to taste. If it looks thin (and tastes thin), add the stock cube or redcurrant jelly. As it thickens, add a glass of red wine. Pour into a jug and place in the warm oven with the plates. Remove the bacon from the birds after about 15 minutes if it is looking crisp, and let the birds brown for the final 5 minutes, but be quick about it and do not let the oven temperature fall. If you can resist the temptation to eat it on the spot, put that, too, into the warm oven.

Partridge hot pot

AN IRISH OR NORTH of England hot pot of any kind is a wonderful dish on cold wet days. Substituting partridge for lamb gives it something extra for a family lunch or a smart dinner party. Use wine with the stock if you are entertaining, but cider if it's just the family. This recipe serves 4 hearty appetites.

4 partridges
900g/2lb potatoes, cut into 5mm/¼in thick slices
2 tbsp olive oil
50g/2oz butter
2-3 celery sticks, thinly sliced
2-3 leeks, thinly sliced
300ml/10fl oz game bird
(see page 16) or chicken stock
1 large glass of dry white wine or dry cider
1 heaped tbsp plain flour
1 tsp chopped thyme
1 tsp brown sugar
Salt and freshly ground black pepper

Make sure the partridges are tidy. Remove the wings for the stockpot if there is not much to them. Preheat the oven to 170°C/325°F/Gas Mark 3. Put the potato slices into a pan of cold water and bring to the boil for a minute or so. Drain and put aside.

Heat the olive oil in a large stainless-steel pan and fry the birds for about 10 minutes in all to brown on all sides. Then remove them to an ovenproof dish and keep hot in the oven. Add as much of the butter as you need to the oil and juices in the pan and fry the sliced celery and leeks until they soften and turn golden. Add the stock and wine or cider and bring up to the bubble, adding the flour a little at a time to thicken. Use a wooden spoon for that and a stainless-steel slice to scrape all the bits off the bottom. Once that is done you can, if you wish, sweeten with a little brown sugar and add salt and pepper to taste.

Put the birds back into the casserole down into the stock amongst the leeks and celery, and sprinkle with the thyme, then spread the potato slices over the top. Use up any butter left over by dotting it on the potatoes and put the casserole (without a lid) in the oven for about 1½ hours. By then the partridge should be tender and the potatoes soft with golden brown crispy edges.

Partridge with dahl

By COMMON CONSENT partridge and lentils go well together and there are many good recipes for that combination. Remember that the dhal will take a while to prepare and cook and it should be ready to go into the oven with the partridges.

2 tbsp olive oil
50g/2oz butter
4 partridges
115g/4oz fat belly of pork or
    unsmoked bacon, cubed
    if one piece, sliced if
    thick rashers
1 medium onion, finely
    chopped
1 large glass dry white wine
600ml/1 pint stock

For the dahl:
225g/8oz lentils (the large
    green ones are best),
    soaked in water for at
least 1 hour but prefera-
    bly overnight
½ tsp ground turmeric
2 tbsp chopped coriander
Salt
2 medium onions, chopped
227g/8oz tin chopped
    tomatoes or 3-4 fresh
    ones, skinned
1 garlic clove, crushed
1-2 tbsp olive oil or 25g/1oz
    butter or cooking fat
(I have left out the chilli
    that would go into a
    dhal to accompany a
    curried bird)

Drain the lentils, then put them into 1.2 litres/2 pints of boiling water, add the turmeric, coriander and a little salt and let them simmer. In the meantime, fry the onions and garlic in the oil, add the tomatoes and fry gently until all are soft. Then add to the dhal and simmer for 30 minutes.

Preheat the oven to 170°C/325°F/Gas Mark 3. Heat the oil and butter in a large stainless-steel pan and fry the partridges on all sides to get them nicely brown. Remove to a lidded casserole, ideally a large Le Creuset. In the remaining fat (add a little more if needs be), fry the pork until the juices flow, then add the onion and fry until tender and golden. Return the partridges to the pan, add the wine while bringing up to the boil, then add the stock and turn down to simmer. Do not forget to scrape off all the bits sticking to the bottom of the pan and stir them into the stock with a wooden spoon.

Now put the dhal into the Le Creuset casserole, remove the birds from the pan and bury them into the dhal. Add the stock and put the lid on the casserole and put it all into the oven. As ever, cooking time is dependent on the bird. Have a time of about 45 minutes in mind – but don't eat by the clock. Cook until the birds are tender.

Partridge risotto

I LOVE RISOTTOS. Of course you must have good arborio rice – do not bother to try to make a risotto with anything else – but the variety of meat, fish or vegetable you can use is enormous. My favourites are chicken liver or, in the spring, really young, fresh broad beans and peas or, seafood, particularly shrimps, squid and mussels, or mushrooms. And, of course, partridge for something even more substantial. This is my version of a Game to Eat recipe. The basic recipe is the same for all risottos, but if you do try the chicken livers do not overcook them. Chop them into bite-size pieces, fry very lightly at the beginning, remove and reserve in a warm place and add right at the end. Overcook them and they will be like little leather buttons.

The Game to Eat recipe suggests reserving the breasts, slicing them and adding to the risotto when it is well cooked, together with a little rocket and baby spinach as a garnish. I am not much of one for garnishes but you may like it.

2 partridges
1 litre/2 pints hot chicken or
    partridge stock
1 bay leaf
Sprinkle of thyme
6 black peppercorns
2 tbsp olive oil
1 medium onion, finely
    chopped
1 garlic clove, crushed
350ml/12fl oz Arborio rice
1 large glass dry white wine
50g/2oz butter
50g/2oz Parmesan cheese
    shavings
2 tsp chopped parsley
Salt

Start by removing the legs and breasts from the birds. Put the carcasses into 1.5 litres/2½ pints of water in a large saucepan, with the bay leaf, a sprinkle of thyme and the black peppercorns. Bring up to the boil, simmer for 30 minutes, then drain off the stock and keep it warm. Take the meat off the legs and chop it quite small. Slice the breasts and chop them too but not quite so small, and keep them separate.

Heat the olive oil in a fairly deep, heavy pan and gently fry the onion and garlic to a light colour. Add the rice and stir about with a wooden spoon to ensure all of it is coated with oil. Once the oil is all absorbed, add the white wine and as it boils up add a ladle of warm stock. Turn down the heat a little but keep the stock just bubbling, and stir gently with a wooden spoon. As the stock gets absorbed add another ladle of stock, repeating the process until you will find that quite suddenly the grains of rice will puff up and become softened. Do not overdo it and produce a glutinous splodge. If you run out of stock, use a little warm water instead.

While the rice is cooking, gently fry the chopped-up meat in the butter, giving the leg meat a minute or two start over the breast. When the rice is almost done, add the meat to it. Make sure it is all well mixed and cooked through. Some people will add a little butter or even a spoonful of cream. I don't, but try it for yourself.

Sprinkle on the Parmesan and parsley and serve straight from the pan.

Partridge paella

In Majorca and Minorca they have the rather nice idea that paella can be made just as well with game as with seafood. You have to be careful of course, because the meat needs more cooking than fish, but it is always good to have a complete meal in one pot. As with risotto, this basic recipe can be used with rabbit or chicken as well as seafood – especially prawns, squid, clams and mussels. (The Spanish mix meat and fish, so you can too.) I do not add much – if any – salt, but that is a matter of taste. I like the colour and flavour of the saffron, but you may prefer turmeric.

2 partridges, each jointed into 4 pieces, removing the breasts and saving the carcass for the stock
2 tbsp olive oil
175g/6oz chorizo sausage, skinned and sliced
1 medium onion, chopped
2 tomatoes, peeled and chopped
350ml/12fl oz paella rice
2 tbsp peas (optional)

½ tsp powdered saffron
½ tsp paprika

For the stock:
1 bay leaf
Sprig or two of thyme
6 black peppercorns
Any odd bits of celery (optional)
Salt and freshly ground black pepper

Put the carcasses into 1.5 litres/2½ pints of water with the stock ingredients and bring up to the boil. Turn down to simmer for 30 minutes, then drain off the stock and keep it warm on the hob.

Heat the oil in a heavy, deep pan (my favourite stainless-steel one is ideal) and fry the partridge meat and the sliced chorizo sausage. I leave the legs whole but slice each breast into at least two parts. When these are all cooked, remove and put them in a warm place.

Now fry the onion and chopped tomatoes in the same pan. Once the onion is golden, add the rice and let it absorb any oil left in the pan (just as you would for a risotto) but then add all the stock, bring briefly to the boil, turn down to simmer and add the partridge meat and the sausage and leave to simmer for 10 minutes or so before adding the peas (if you are using them), paprika and the saffron. The rice should be cooked in another 5-10 minutes, but that is very variable, depending on the rice. If the stock has all been absorbed before the rice is done (al dente but not soggy), add a little more hot water. If the rice is done before all the stock has been absorbed just turn up the heat a little to evaporate it. Serve directly from the pan.

Partridge tagine with olives and lemon

THEY TELL ME that a tagine is actually a traditional North African conical cooking pot, rather than the dish itself. Rather like a casserole I suppose. Usually over here it seems to be a spicy meat dish, often with apricots. This recipe was brought back from Morocco by Debby Mason. Serve with boiled rice or couscous. Serves 6.

2 tbsp olive oil
6 partridges
3 medium onions, sliced
1 good pinch of saffron
    threads
1 tbsp chopped garlic
1 tsp ground cumin
1 tsp ground ginger
1 tsp paprika
1 tsp turmeric
1 tsp ground cinnamon
2 cinnamon sticks
1 pinch cayenne pepper

600ml/1 pint game bird
    stock (see page 16) or
    chicken stock
125ml/4fl oz fresh lemon juice
1 large preserved lemon,
    pipped and sliced
175g/6oz pitted green and
    black olives
1 small bunch of flat leaf
    parsley, chopped
1 small bunch of coriander,
    chopped
Salt

Preheat the oven to 180°C/350°F/Gas Mark 4. Heat the oil in a large heavy casserole with a good well-fitting lid and gently fry the partridges until browned on all sides, about 10 minutes in all. Remove them and set aside. Then fry the onions gently in the fat and oil until soft and golden. Stir in the spices with a wooden spoon, mixing them well into the onions, and fry for another couple of minutes. Enjoy the wonderful smell of all that! Debby says it takes her back to Jemaa El Fna in Marrakesh, where the spice sellers rub shoulders with snake charmers, dodgy dentists, herbalists, gulli-gulli men and acrobats.

Forgetting all that, and getting back to the kitchen, return the partridges to the casserole, add the stock and lemon juice and bring to the boil, then turn down to simmer slowly, with the lid partly on, for 20 minutes, giving it a stir now and again with a wooden spoon. Stir in the lemon slices and olives with a wooden spoon, put the lid on firmly and put in the oven for 20-30 minutes or until the partridges are cooked through but still just pink. Check the seasoning, sprinkle with the chopped parsley and coriander and serve.

Debby says she sometimes adds a couple of teaspoons of ras el hanout – a Moroccan blend of at least a dozen spices, sometimes thirty or forty – if you can find some in your local souk.

'Damned silly bird the
duck. Too much for one
and not enough for
two'

Duck

Anas platrhynchos

Wild duck (Mallard), 98

Crumbed roast duck, 100

Roast or grilled duck breasts
with a fruit sauce, 102

Duck leg stew, 104

Wild duck (Mallard)

Season (UK): 1st September–20th February (below tide)
Elsewhere 31st January

THE MALLARD IS by far our best-known wild duck.
Breeding in Europe, North America, Asia, New Zealand
and Australia, and migrating even further afield, its social
habits are not unlike those of many humans. Fathers play
no part in bringing up the young. They cross-breed
with – and threaten the survival as separate species of – a
number of attractive rare ducks. Avoiding controversy (as
is my way), I will only mention that the Mallard seems to
have the highest rate of male homosexuality of any bird,
and pass on my way to consideration of the Mallard in
the kitchen.

I do not find that wild ducks are the easiest birds to
cook well. Unlike the domesticated puddle ducks, which
are very fat, wild ducks are leaner and more muscular. I
recollect one night when I was navigating a Second World
War York freighter (which had wings and Merlin engines
of a Lancaster bomber attached to a more capacious
body) across the Sahara from Nigeria to Libya that we
collided with an unfortunate duck coming the other way.
The bird flew straight into the radiator of one of the four
Merlin engines, which then overheated by the time we

reached Tripoli. Even without the hazard of aircraft bumbling along through the night at 180 knots at 6,000 to 10,000ft, that crossing must be quite a challenge to even a muscular duck.

These recipes are all based on Mallard, which is really the only wild duck you are likely to find in the shop. I once used Mandarin Duck, which were shot in error from a flock of about twenty that were taken for very high Mallard. If you are lucky enough to acquire any Teal, they will look and cook very much like Mallard.

The difficult bit if you are cooking wild duck whole (particularly roasting) is to avoid either drying up the breasts or undercooking the legs. One answer is to cook them separately. Another is to coat them with a breadcrumb crust, and I give recipes for both options. The casserole or stew of the duck legs I find particularly good.

That apart, there is one other difficulty with wild duck. As an aristocratic London clubman (I cannot remember who) said, 'Damned silly bird the duck. Too much for one and not enough for two.'

Crumbed roast duck

I RECOMMEND REMOVING the legs from these ducks to make the duck stew on page 104, or indeed simply to fry with onion, herbs and crushed garlic, to eat as an hors-d'oeuvre. Of the options for roasting I prefer the crumb casing. Indeed I think casing almost any fowl or meat in a butter/herb/breadcrumb jacket adds something extra to the sight, smell and taste of the dish. Some years ago I adapted this recipe from a favourite Sophie Grigson one for rack of lamb with a herb crust. Choose your fruit flavour. The favourite flavouring is probably orange, but try others too, such as dried or fresh apricots or dates, or quarters of apple.

2 oranges
2 ducks, legs removed and
    reserved (see introduction)
140g/5oz butter, softened
140g/5oz fresh white
    breadcrumbs

1 garlic clove, crushed
Herbs of your choice, lots
    of them, chopped
Salt and freshly ground
    black pepper

Preheat the oven to 230°C/450°F/Gas Mark 8. Finely grate the zest of one of the oranges and squeeze the juice. Slice the second orange into rounds. Butter the inside of the duck with no more than 25g/1oz of the butter and smear a little more on the outside of the birds. Put as many orange rounds (according to size) as seems sensible into the bird cavities. That is, you are not stuffing them – just adding flavour. Alternatively, use apricots, dates or apples.

Soften the rest of the butter and work into the bread-crumbs to get a sticky mixture together with the garlic and herbs. Add the orange zest and juice and season with salt and pepper. Plaster the birds with the crumb mixture, then put them on a roasting rack in a roasting tin and cook in the oven for 30 minutes or so until done, but the breast should be pink.

Roast or grilled duck breasts with a fruit sauce

IF YOU ARE COOKING for four adults with light appetites – or serving the dish as a first course – one breast each would do nicely but as a main course for healthy appetites I would be tempted to do two breasts per person. You can make the sauce well ahead of time – but keep it warm until you are ready to use it. If you buy whole ducks, you will have the legs for a duck stew (see page 104) and the carcasses for stock.

450g/1lb blackcurrants or ripe plums, halved and stoned
1 cinnamon stick
1 glass of dry white wine
1 tbsp wine vinegar
Sugar, to taste – preferably caster but granulated will do
4 duck breasts
Olive oil, for brushing
Salt and freshly ground black pepper

Put the blackcurrants or plums, cinnamon, white wine and wine vinegar into a saucepan. Let it come briefly to the boil, then turn down to just simmer gently until the fruit is really soft. Pour into a stainless-steel sieve and push it through with a wooden spoon into the saucepan, add the sugar and heat until it dissolves into the fruit. Add black pepper to taste – I use quite a lot. Keep the sauce warm over a gentle heat while you cook the duck.

For roasting, preheat the oven to 220°C/425°F/Gas Mark 7. Brush the breasts with oil and lay them cut-side down on a roasting rack in a roasting tin. Put plenty of salt and pepper on the skin side and cook for 10 minutes if the breasts are on the thin side, or a few minutes more to make sure they are cooked – but still just pink. Alternatively, grill under a very hot grill for 5 minutes a side, or a bit more if you like them well done.

When cooked, let the breasts rest for a minute or two in a warm oven (if you don't have one simply leave the oven door open) then serve surrounded by sauce.

Duck leg stew

FOR EVERY DUCK breast there is a duck leg and half a carcass for stock and you can make this as simple or as exotic as you like. The legs do make a rather tasty stew or casserole. If you can't find the canned beans you want use some well-soaked dry ones – or lentils etc. – all available at Waitrose or other good supermarkets. This recipe serves 4 as a first course or light lunch.

For the stock:
2 duck carcasses
6-8 peppercorns
1 celery stick, chopped
1 bay leaf, some parsley and
    thyme as per your taste
1 onion, chopped, or 2
    shallots, chopped in half
1 large or 2 small carrots,
    roughly chopped

For the stew:
4 duck legs
Plain flour, enough to cover
    the duck legs
25g/1oz butter
115g/4oz streaky bacon,
    chopped

2 shallots, chopped
2 carrots, chopped
300ml/10fl oz red wine
Selection of herbs, e.g.
    thyme, parsley,
    marjoram
200g/7oz can chopped
    tomatoes
½ x 400g/14oz can (or a
    small can, if you can
    find it) flageolet or
    cannellini beans or
    lentils, drained and
    rinsed
Salt and freshly ground
    black pepper

To make the stock, put all the ingredients in a saucepan and cover with water. Bring to the boil, then simmer gently with the lid on for ½ hour, skimming off any scum with a slotted spoon at intervals. Allow to cool, then strain and measure out 450ml/16fl oz. Any surplus can be frozen like ice cubes.

Preheat the oven to 170°C/325°F/Gas Mark 3 (unless you intend to cook the stew on the hob, see below). Season the flour, then roll the duck legs in it. Melt the butter in a large stainless-steel pan (with a lid if available) and briefly fry the legs and bacon, then put them aside. Fry the shallots and carrots in the remaining fat. Add the wine, reserved stock, herbs, tomatoes and beans. Return the duck legs and bacon bits to the pan. Bring it all up to the boil, season to taste with salt and pepper, then reduce to a slow simmer. If you have used a deep pan with a lid, you can either leave it to simmer on the hob for 45 minutes or put it all into a casserole in the oven.

*'The grouse season opens on
the 12th of August –
The Glorious Twelfth!'*

Grouse

Lagopus lagopus

Grouse

PERHAPS THE GREATEST of all British game birds, the Red Grouse was once widespread not only in Scotland but also on the English moorlands as far south as Dartmoor and Exmoor. Sadly, human population pressures have all but eliminated grouse from England. Although there is a surviving Welsh population, with reports of Welsh birds crossing the Bristol Channel to Exmoor, the tide is running against the grouse except where positive measures are taken to protect its habitat and control its predators.

The Black Grouse *(Tetrao tetrix)* is far less common than the Red. It is both bigger and heavier, but, like the Red, has been the victim of human pressures on its habitat of ancient pinewoods.

The grouse season opens in the UK on 12th August – the 'Glorious Twelfth' – and it is the bird's status as our premier game bird that ensures its survival. The grouse moors are valuable estate and well maintained by their owners. The income from shooting finances the control (but not elimination) of predators, but the grouse are truly wild birds. They are beautifully camouflaged and fly fast and low. They are challenging birds to shoot and, of course, excellent to eat.

Roast grouse

THERE IS REALLY only one way to cook grouse. That is simply roast and eaten either hot or cold. Jane Grigson suggests putting fruit inside the bird – bananas, raspberries, cranberries or grapes. Sophie is all for serving them with bread sauce (something for which I have never found much use at all). For my part, I think it best to keep it really simple – especially as I usually finish up with the carcass in my fingers.

You may wish to have some vegetables, although they can just get in the way of unrestrained grouse guzzling. Probably the best accompaniment would be braised red cabbage.

A little lemon juice
55g/2oz butter, softened
4 grouse
8 or 12 fat belly of pork or
    unsmoked bacon rashers
2 tbsp olive oil

4 thick slices of good white
    bread for crumbs, 2 tbsp
    per bird
Watercress, to garnish
Cranberry, rowan or red
    currant jelly, to serve

Preheat the oven to 190°C/375°F/Gas Mark 5. Add a drop or two (no more) of lemon juice to the softened butter and smear it around the inside of each bird. Cover with the pork rashers, using 2 or 3 per bird – cocktail sticks help to keep them in place. Put the birds on a roasting rack in a roasting tin and roast for 25-35 minutes, then remove the bacon/pork and put the birds back to brown for another 10 minutes. (If you prefer to roast hotter and quicker, then use 220°C/425°F/Gas Mark 7 for 25 minutes.)

If you have the grouse livers, you can let them cook inside the birds and then remove them. That can be fiddly and it can be easier simply to take them out before you cook the bird and fry them very quickly before you fry the bread.

So – while the birds are finishing browning – heat the olive oil in a large frying pan and fry the bread to use as croutons. (You may need to do this in batches.) Then just brown the breadcrumbs in the hot oil.

Remove the birds from the oven. Set them on the croutons with the livers softened to a paste. Garnish with watercress, sprinkle with the fried breadcrumbs and serve with the cranberry, rowan or redcurrant jelly.

'A beautiful bird, but
 not in my garden or
 in crops'

Wood Pigeon
Columba palumbus

Wood pigeon

Season: All the year round

SADLY, FOR IT IS a handsome bird, the wood pigeon is by
virtue of its numbers a pest and is shot all year round.
The more we observe birds, the less apt the pejorative
expression 'bird brain' seems to be. Wood pigeons are not
easy to shoot in flight with a shotgun: they recognise men
carrying guns and will often keep out of range. Even
when the chance of a good overhead shot presents itself,
the wary pigeon often seems to detect the flash of the gun
and jinks like a bomber caught in the searchlights avoiding the flak. I never feel a day's shooting is quite complete
without getting a wood pigeon.

They can be as much a pest in the garden (particularly
the vegetable patch) as in a wheatfield, and I use a .22
compressed air rifle from the bedroom window – when I

get the chance. All too often, however, the wary wood pigeon is up and away before I have unlatched, let alone opened, the window.

At a maximum weight of about 550g/1¼lb (including a crop packed full of wheat or barley), there is not a lot to eat on a pigeon, but whether you just take the breasts and leave the rest for the local fox, or whether you use the whole bird, the wood pigeon is good food – although you need one per head.

Pigeon with cabbage

PIGEON IS NOT A delicate flavour and since you can never be quite sure how old the birds are, slow cooking with cabbage brings out the best in them. I do not think this dish really needs other vegetables, but if you are feeding hungry teenagers, jacket potatoes never go amiss – and steamed carrots.

4 pigeons
2-3 tbsp olive oil
4 rashers unsmoked fat
    bacon, chopped
2 medium onions, chopped
1 really large red, green or
    savoy (my favourite)
    cabbage – or better still
    2 small ones, cored and
    sliced thinly
2 Bramley apples, peeled,

cored and chopped
150ml/5fl oz red wine
150ml/5fl oz game bird
    stock (see page 16) or
    chicken stock
1 tsp chopped raisins
    (optional)
1 tsp soft brown sugar
    (optional)
Salt and freshly ground
    black pepper

Preheat the oven to 170°C/325°F/Gas Mark 3. Remove the breasts, legs and wings from the birds (reserve the carcasses for a stock or soup base), in a similar way to jointing a pheasant.

Heat the oil in a deep stainless-steel pan. Start the bacon frying gently, then fry the pigeon pieces. Do not overdo them. When they are nicely brown, transfer them to a warm place. Fry the onions in the remaining juices, then the cabbage, then the apples, using the rest of the oil if the cabbage has absorbed all that is in the pan. Season with salt and pepper, and add the raisins or sugar if you like a touch of sweetness. You can either put the pigeon pieces on top of the cabbage etc. in the big stainless-steel pan if it has a good lid, or put it all into an earthenware casserole with a tight-fitting lid. Add the red wine and stock and let it cook for at least 1½ hours.

Fried pigeon breasts

THERE ARE MANY good cooks, Clarissa Dickson Wright of Two Fat Ladies fame was amongst them, who reckon you can simply fry pigeon breasts and serve them direct from the pan. Well, you can if you are satisfied that they come from a young pigeon, but every now and again you are bound to find you have something it is best to slip under the table to the dog.

Clarissa suggested just rolling the breasts in flour seasoned with paprika, salt and pepper, and dry mustard powder and frying in butter for 5 minutes a side. If they are young, that is fine and if you like you could pour some thick cream into the pan as the breasts are almost done, add a drop of lemon juice and serve on fresh hot toast, but check the bird's birth certificate first!

Casseroled pigeon breasts

FOR THIS RECIPE you use just the breasts (making stock from the remaining carcasses) which makes the actual eating business rather simple, as opposed to picking up the bird and chewing it. As for vegetables, as always I would go for either jacket potatoes or mashed and creamed with celeriac or, in season, really new potatoes and whichever vegetables are seasonally at their best.

25g/1oz butter
2 tbsp olive oil
4 pigeons, either cooked whole or just the 8 breasts removed and cooked separately
12 small onions – the really little ones, the size of quails' eggs – or shallots
225g/8oz unsmoked back

bacon rashers
225g/8oz mushrooms, the chestnut variety are ideal
150ml/5fl oz pigeon or chicken stock
1 large glass of red wine
2 tbsp brandy
Salt and freshly ground black pepper

Preheat the oven to 170°C/325°F/Gas Mark 3. Heat the butter and oil in a large, deep, stainless-steel pan and brown the breasts or birds, then remove them to a lidded Le Creuset casserole using a slotted spoon. Lightly brown the onions, bacon and mushrooms. Add the onions and mushrooms around the birds and put the bacon over them. Season with salt and pepper.

Bring the stock up to the boil in the frying pan, scraping off the bottom any bits that may have stuck and incorporating them into the liquid. Add the wine then, as it all comes back to the boil, add the brandy and pour the lot over the birds. Put on the lid and put into the oven to cook. If the birds are young, this should take about 1 hour – but be prepared to give them another half hour if needs be. (You can use a fork to test it, or cut a bit off and try it.) Check after half an hour's cooking to make sure that it is not drying out, and add more stock if needs be.

Complete pigeon casserole

THIS IS A GOOD way of cooking those pigeons that might be beyond their first flush of youth. It will feed four people with modest appetites. I think it goes well with jacket potatoes (but you'll need a double oven as they really need to be cooked at 200°C/400°F/Gas Mark 6), but mashed potatoes are good too and carrots or broccoli will add some extra colour.

2 good-sized pigeons, cut in half length-wise using a pair of poultry scissors (see below)
50g/2oz butter
225g/8oz fat belly of pork (you can use bacon rashers but they won't be nearly so good), cut into 1cm/½in cubes
2-3 shallots or 1 medium onion, thinly sliced

1 large garlic clove, chopped
115g/4oz mushrooms (preferably portabellini, chestnut or wild field mushrooms), sliced
300ml/10fl oz dark ale or red wine
300ml/10fl oz game bird stock (see page 16) or chicken stock
1 bouquet garni (see page 18)
Salt and ground black pepper

Preheat the oven to 180°C/350°F/Gas Mark 4. Take your poultry scissors and start from the back end of the bird, cutting along the line of the breast bone right to the neck cavity. Then pull the two sides of the bird apart and sever along the line of the backbone into the two halves.

Melt the butter in an ovenproof casserole (I also use my favourite big stainless-steel lidded pan) and fry the pork cubes and pigeon pieces. Once they are browned, set them aside on a plate and gently fry the shallots with the garlic and mushrooms. Add the dark ale, stock and bouquet garni and bring to the boil for a moment while you scrape those good bits off the bottom of the pan, then return the pigeons, put on a well-fitting lid and cook in the oven for 1 hour or until the birds are tender.

Pigeon breasts with fruit sauce

With every respect to Clarissa Dickson Wright, who liked pigeon breasts unadorned, I think that they can be improved with a fruit sauce – and my favourite is a blackberry one.

On their own, as in this recipe, these pigeon breasts make an excellent quick brunch, but if served with winter vegetables such as carrots and potatoes mashed with celeriac or a summer salad of rocket, beetroot leaves, baby spinach, spring onions, tomatoes and fresh boiled beetroot, they will make a main meal.

1-2 tbsp olive oil
8 pigeon breasts
300ml/10fl oz game bird stock (see page 16) or chicken stock

2 tbsp white wine vinegar or white wine
4 tbsp redcurrant jelly
Little plain flour, for thickening
225g/8oz blackberries

Pour the olive oil on to a deep plate and quickly turn the pigeon breasts in it. Sear them on a hot griddle pan – Le Creuset, as always, is best – for about 2 minutes a side, then remove from the pan and reserve in a warm place covered with foil.

Add the stock and the wine vinegar to the pan, initially bringing the liquid to the boil, to scrape up any juices and burnt bits from the pigeon breasts.

As it begins to reduce, lower the heat a little and add the redcurrant jelly, stirring it in with a wooden spoon to dissolve. Once it begins to thicken (and you can hasten that by adding some flour but only a shake or two of flour from a flour shaker, not by spoonfuls) add the blackberries and let them cook until they are soft.

Slice the warm pigeon breasts, put them back on their warm dish and pour the blackberry sauce over them.

Pigeon risotto

YOU CAN MAKE a good risotto with a wide variety of meats (and indeed seafood) and elsewhere in the book I have a recipe for partridge risotto.

However, I regard pigeons as such pests in gardens, parks and farms that I am always pleased to eat them and in a risotto is a good way to do so. It is however absolutely necessary to use really good Arborio rice and, as with so much else, I buy mine from Waitrose. Serves 4.

4 pigeons
Olive oil
300g/10oz Arborio rice
1 glass white wine
1 medium onion, finely
    chopped
1 clove garlic, crushed
1 rasher fat back bacon
2 tbsp olive oil

1 tbsp grated Parmesan

For the stock:
The legs and carcasses of the
    pigeons
1 bay leaf
Sprinkle of thyme
6 peppercorns

Start by removing the breasts from the birds and putting to one side.

Then dismember the birds, removing the legs breaking the carcass into two and put those into a saucepan with the bay leaf, thyme, peppercorns and a little pepper and salt. Add about 1 litre/2 pints of water.

Bring to the boil, reduce to a simmer for about 30 minutes. Drain off the stock and keep warm.

Meanwhile slice the breasts, chop them and cook gently with a little olive oil in a pan until tender and reserve.

Now heat the 2 tablespoons of the olive oil in a large, fairly deep, heavy pan. Gently fry the chopped onion and chopped bacon and garlic to a light brown.

Add the rice and stir it about to ensure that it is coated with the remaining oil.

Once that is absorbed add the glass of white wine which should boil up with a satisfying sizzle.

As it boils away add a ladle of the stock turning down the heat to keep the stock just bubbling and as each ladleful is absorbed add the next. Keep the rice from sticking by stirring gently with a wooden spoon.

Quite suddenly, after 15 to 20 minutes or so, the rice will puff up and soften. If you should run out of stock in this process, just add warm water, but do not overcook the rice or it will become a nasty sticky mess.

Just as the rice puffs up, add the chopped pigeon breasts and sprinkle with the Parmesan.

Then serve directly from the pan at the table.

'A beautiful bird – but
don't let my sentimentality
put you off eating it'

Woodcock

Scolopax rusticola

Woodcock

Season: 2nd October-31st January in England
1st September-31st January in Scotland

THE WOODCOCK IS a little smaller than a wood pigeon. Living in woodlands, particularly those on boggy or soft soil, and being wonderfully camouflaged, woodcocks will scarcely be seen by town dwellers. Unless you almost tread on the bird, putting it up to flight, you could walk unknowingly past one. In flight it is made quite distinctive by the noisy beat of its broad wings, its swift flight through the trees and, of course, its long, slightly curved back.

It is said that 40,000 pairs of woodcock breed in Britain and come here during the winter – especially if it is cold in mainland Europe when large numbers of migrants exploit the cold easterly winds to cross the North Sea to shelter in our woodlands.

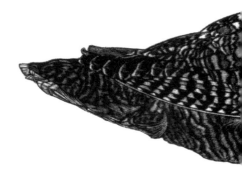

They are good to eat, but I have to confess to a touch of sentimental weakness. In most places that I shoot there are not a lot of woodcock, and it is such a beautiful bird with such a graceful flight and half melancholy call, that I just cannot find the will to shoot them.

However, if you find it at the butcher's, or are given one, do not let my sentimentality put you off eating it – I wouldn't be. There is only one way to cook this bird – roast it, but let it hang for 5-6 days first.

Roast woodcock on toast

WOODCOCK SHOULD be cooked whole – with the head on. Remove the crop and gizzard before cooking, but leave the trail (liver, heart and intestines) where it is.

4 woodcocks
4 pieces of pork fat, enough
    to cover the birds
4 slices of white bread

Lemon juice, to taste
4 tsp brandy
Salt and freshly ground
    pepper

Preheat the oven to 230°C/450°F/Gas Mark 8. Cover each bird with a piece of pork fat and put them on a roasting rack in a roasting tin. It will be done in 18-20 minutes.

Take the birds out of the oven, remove each bird's trail and in a small, warm saucepan, mash it and mix with a good squeeze of lemon juice, brandy and some salt and pepper. Meanwhile, toast the bread. Spread the mixture on the toast, put a bird on top of each one and eat while hot.

'The king of game'

Deer

Cervidae family

Deer

Season (UK): Slightly complicated. Wild venison is in season from September to the end of February, but farmed venison is in the shops all year round

THERE ARE SIX species of deer in Britain – all of which make good eating. The epitome of all deer is, of course, the Red Deer *(Cervus elaphus)*. A true native of these islands, it is now mostly confined to Scotland and the moors of southwestern England. The Roe Deer *(Capreolus capreolus)* was also indigenous but hunted to extinction in the 17th century, then reintroduced and is now widely spread (some gardeners looking at their roses would say too widely spread).

The Fallow Deer *(Dama dama)* – perhaps the prettiest of them all – was also originally a native species, but after it was driven out by the Ice Age it was not reintroduced until after the Norman Conquest. The Sika *(Cervus nippon)* was introduced from the Far East in 1806 and (attractive as it is) is now posing a problem since it can breed with our Red Deer.

The Muntjac *(Muntiacus reevesi)* and the Water Deer *(Hydropotes Inermis inermis)*, sometimes called Chinese Water (or River) Deer, are both small deer fairly recently introduced. The Muntjac is sometimes called the pig deer (although it barks rather like a dog) and causes a lot of destruction in woodlands, whilst the Water Deer is a very early species, having no antlers and relying on its tusks for defence. The good news about all six species is that they each provide venison. The sad news is that, particularly in the south of England (notably Sussex), numbers have increased to the point that they inflict serious damage to crops and woodlands, not to mention gardens. Where population pressures are greatest, deer migrate quite widely, crossing busy roads, particularly at night. Both humans and deer suffer casualties. Something like 30-50,000 deer out of a population of around 1 million are currently killed on the road every year, and it has become necessary to cull herds to reduce the danger of vehicle/deer collisions.

I love venison. Do not be put off by those people (generally who have never eaten it) who say it is too gamey. It is far more likely to be lacking flavour because it has not been hung long enough. Generally speaking it is cooked like beef (and to be really good, beef should be hung for 3 to 4 weeks in the butcher's cool room). It is leaner than beef so needs even more care in cooking.

The recipe for roasting a whole haunch in flour and water paste you could adapt for any large joint. Otherwise (especially with small 1.3-2.25kg/3-5lb roasting joints), it is wise to marinate overnight before cooking to avoid drying out.

Generally you can do most things with venison that you might have done with beef.

Simple roast venison

A GOOD BUTCHER will be able to supply venison for roasting already boned and rolled. Remember it is lean meat so it is healthy eating but also needs careful cooking because of the lack of fat. I would always recommend marinating overnight. For a normal-sized joint, I would make a half quantity of the marinade for the Roast Haunch of Venison opposite.

It is also well worthwhile larding the joint with thin strips of bacon fat known as lardons and wrapping it in a fatty piece of pork skin, if you can get it from your butcher.

Cook the joint at 180°C/350°F/Gas Mark 4 for 20 minutes per 450g/1lb plus 20 minutes. Bigger joints need proportionally less time: say 15 minutes per 450g/1lb plus 15 minutes for a joint of 2.25kg/5lb. Do not overcook venison: like good beef if it is well hung it is best a little pink.

There will not be much in the pan from which to make gravy, so you might like a sauce. Venison goes with port wine, redcurrant jelly, orange or lemon, cinnamon and allspice. Choose the ingredients to suit yourself, but Jane Grigson recommends Queen Victoria's favourite, which is very simple and is included below.

2 tbsp port (which I thought too little)
1 small stick of cinnamon

225g/8oz redcurrant jelly (which I found too much)
Zest of 1 lemon

Just put the ingredients together into a pan, gently warm and stir together with a wooden spoon.

Roast haunch of venison

THE ROAST HAUNCH of venison has been a classic English dish for the last thousand years at least. It was served, no doubt in style, in castles, great houses and bishops' palaces and, in secret, in humble homes under threat of dire punishment for taking deer. Nowadays it is only the problem of finding a butcher who will sell you a haunch (and the cash to pay him) that need hold you back. The size will very greatly from the Muntjac to the magnificent Red, so you might have a very large, or quite small, haunch. That need not affect the marinade but you might need more or less flour and water paste for the jacket.

When I was a minister in Margaret Thatcher's Government, ministers were, from time to time, offered a haunch from the deer culled in the Royal Parks, an offer I could not bring myself to refuse even though the only place to hang it in our London home was the bathroom.

The haunch needs to be marinated for 24 hours before cooking. As for the vegetables, potatoes – new or mashed – creamed with celeriac, French beans or broad beans, all go well.

1 haunch of venison, hung for 7-10 days
Knob of butter
115g/4oz pork fat, cut into thin strips, known as lardons
450g/1lb plain flour, and a

little for the gravy
57g/2oz suet
2 carrots, split lengthwise
1 onion, quartered (or several small shallots)
1 celery stick, chopped

For the marinade:
600ml/1 pint red wine
2 tbsp olive oil
4 tbsp red wine vinegar
4 medium onions, sliced
2 celery sticks
2 large (or 4 small) carrots,
    sliced

1 bay leaf
12 black peppercorns
12 juniper berries
4 garlic cloves, crushed
1 tsp chopped thyme
Zest of ¼ orange

Put all the marinade ingredients in a large lidded container and mix together. Put the venison in, cover and leave to marinate for 24 hours.

Preheat the oven to 170°C/325°F/Gas Mark 3. Remove the venison from the marinade (saving it for the gravy) and make sure it's well dried. Rub the butter into the meat. Using a larding needle, thread the lardons of pork fat into the venison – or with a sharp knife, cut incisions and squeeze in the pieces of fat. Put the flour and suet in a bowl, mix with enough water to make a really sticky paste with which to plaster the haunch, using your hands to do so (you may need more or less than this according to the size of your haunch). Cover the venison completely with the paste, sealing it inside. Then wrap it all in grease-proof paper and tie up with string.

Put the haunch on a roasting rack in a large roasting tin. Cover the floor of the tin with boiling water and cook in the oven for 4-5 hours according to size. (A starting guess would be about 15 minutes per 450g/1lb.) About halfway through the cooking time, at which stage the juices should have dripped through the paste jacket, put the vegetables under the rack, topping up the water if need be.

Half an hour before the estimated cooking time, remove the venison from the oven and remove the paste jacket. This will let you check with a carving fork to see how well done the meat is and give an idea of when to start the vegetables.

Venison needs to be served good and hot (or completely cold), so it is best at this stage to set the haunch on one side for a moment or two, pour some boiling water into the roasting tin, put it over a high heat on the hob, scrape up all the burned bits, pour them into a saucepan and then return the joint to the roasting tin and into the oven as quickly as possible to resume cooking. You can make the gravy in the saucepan, thicken up with flour and add some of the marinade for extra flavour and colour.

Venison steaks

JUST LIKE BEEF steaks, venison steaks can be grilled, fried or, if the weather is right, barbecued. It is no bad idea to tenderise and bring out the flavour of venison steaks by marinating them for at least 2 hours, preferably 4 hours.

4 venison steaks, whatever
   size you fancy

Marinade:
150ml/5fl oz red wine
1 tbsp olive oil
1 small onion, chopped
2 garlic cloves, crushed

1 dessertspoon English
   mustard
1 tbsp brown sugar (if you
   like your barbecue
   marinade sweet) or a
   little chilli powder
   sprinkled on the steaks
   (if you like it hot)

Mix the marinade ingredients well, add the steaks, cover and leave to marinate for 2-4 hours. Drain the steaks well before cooking. If you are barbecuing them, you can use the marinade during cooking to prevent the outside from burning before the steak is done. Personally I prefer to use a really heavy Le Creuset skillet in the comfort of my kitchen, and to eat my steak slightly crisp on the outside and pink in the middle.

Minute venison fillet steaks

THIS RECIPE I HAVE borrowed from my friends in the Game To Eat campaign by The Countryside Alliance and The National Game Dealers' Association. If you use one of those splendid Le Creuset heavy skillets you need not use the butter: just brush the pan and the steaks with olive oil and keep the cholesterol down. This will go well with a mixed rocket, watercress and baby spinach salad. You will find that ready-prepared in Waitrose or other good supermarkets.

4 venison fillet steaks

Sauce:
2 tbsp port
225g/8oz redcurrant jelly

15g/½oz butter
1 tbsp olive oil
115g/4oz Somerset Brie
Salt and freshly ground
black pepper

Gently warm the port in a small pan, dissolve the redcurrant jelly into it, and keep warm over a low heat.

If the steaks are thick, put them on a wooden board, cover with kitchen paper or cling film and bash them with a wooden rolling pin to reduce to about 1cm/½in thick to tenderise them.

Melt the butter in the oil in a heavy pan, season the steaks with salt and pepper to taste and cook (but do not over-cook!). Serve with a slice of Brie on each steak – (I think it best to put the Brie on the steak in the pan just before it is done) and a little of the port and redcurrant sauce.

Venison casserole
with beer

IT USED TO BE that no one wanted shoulder of venison, but I fear the word has got out that like those less popular cuts of beef (my favourite is shin) it makes an excellent casserole or stew. There are as many recipes for venison casserole as there are cooks, but these two approaches – one with beer, an 'after a winter day in the garden or shooting' style – and the other more suitable for a dinner party.

I enjoy jacket potatoes with this casserole but of course you will need two ovens for that, as they would never cook at 150°C/300°F/Gas Mark 2 and microwaved jacket potatoes are, at the best, a waste of good food. My second choice would be mashed potatoes or creamed potatoes and celeriac (see page 19) with steamed carrots and/or Brussels sprouts or, if you prefer, buttered swede.

900g/2lb shoulder of
   venison, cut into
   2.5cm/1in cubes
2 tbsp plain flour,
   seasoned
2 tbsp olive oil
2 medium onions, chopped
2 garlic cloves, chopped
4 carrots, diced
225g/8oz piece of

unsmoked streaky bacon,
   diced
4 really small turnips
1 bouquet garni
   (see page 18)
300ml/10fl oz warm
   venison or beef stock
300ml/10fl oz dark ale
Salt and freshly ground
   black pepper

Preheat the oven to 150°C/300°F/Gas Mark 2. Put a dish in to warm. Turn the diced venison in the seasoned flour. Heat the oil in either that stainless-steel pan or a lidded Le Creuset casserole, fry the venison until browned on all sides – about 5 minutes. You may find this easier to do in two or three batches. Remove the meat on to the warm dish using a slotted spoon to leave the oil in the pan.

Fry the onions, garlic, carrots and bacon in the remaining oil until the onions are golden brown. Add the warm stock, then, as it approaches the boil, add the ale. Let it just come to the boil, then turn down to a gentle simmer. Stir in the meat then scrape up and incorporate all those lovely bits stuck on the bottom of the pan using a stainless-steel slice. Add the bouquet garni, the turnips, if available, and season well with black pepper. Cover with the lid and transfer to the oven for about 2-2½ hours, depending on the quality and age of the venison.

Remember if you want to eat at 7.30pm you can put this in the oven 3-4 hours earlier, then remove it from the oven after 1½ hours to check how it is going and return for the last hour and a half to be finished at 7.30pm.

Venison casserole with red wine

THERE ARE SOME magnificently complicated recipes for a venison casserole. Robert Carrier's Magdalen Venison is probably the greatest of them all. I confess I have not yet made it – but one day or day and a half I will. In the meantime, this is my workaday recipe to which you may like to add some extras, but I think it is good enough not just for the family Saturday dinner but for a dinner party too. I usually serve this with creamed potatoes and celeriac (see page 19) or jacket potatoes and a favourite green vegetable in season.

900g/2lb shoulder of
   venison, diced
115g/4oz piece of streaky
   bacon, cut into
   5-10mm/¼-½in cubes
2 tbsp plain flour, seasoned
300ml/10fl oz hot venison
   or beef stock
1 tbsp olive oil
25g/1oz butter
1 medium onion, chopped
1 celery stick, chopped into
   5-10mm/¼-½in pieces
1 carrot, diced
1 garlic clove, crushed
150ml/5fl oz red wine

115g/4oz flat mushrooms,
   such as portabellini or
   chestnut
1 bouquet garni (see page 18)
Salt and freshly ground
   black pepper

For the marinade:
150ml/5fl oz red wine
1 tbsp olive oil
1 tbsp brandy
1 medium onion, chopped
6 black peppercorns
Peel of a quarter of an
   orange, in strips

Put all the marinade ingredients in a large lidded container or basin to be covered with cling film and mix together. Add the venison, cover and leave to marinate for 5-6 hours at least, but preferably overnight.

Preheat the oven to 170°C/325°F/Gas Mark 3. Remove the venison from the marinade (saving it for the sauce), dry on kitchen paper, then toss or roll it in seasoned flour. Have the hot stock ready for use.

Heat the oil and butter in a deep stainless-steel pan. Start the bacon frying and then add the onion, celery, carrot and garlic. As the bacon and vegetables begin to brown, add the venison which will rapidly take up the oil and butter, so turn the heat down a little and keep turning the meat over to avoid burning. As it really dries out, add the marinade and bring up to the boil, then add the red wine and as much stock as it needs to keep the meat and vegetables covered and reduce to a simmer.

Now you can add the mushrooms. I leave it to this stage partly because if you fry them they will simply soak up all the butter and oil in an instant and the meat will not have enough in which to fry. If you add more to satisfy the mushrooms, they will release it later in the cooking and your casserole will be too oily. Adding them at this stage will let them cook slowly and they will take up any spare oil too.

If your pan is suitable and has a good lid, you could let it simmer on top of the cooker for 1½-2 hours, or until the venison is tender. Otherwise, put the pan (if it is ovenproof, if not, tip it all into a casserole) in the oven for 1½-2 hours.

Venison meatballs with tomato sauce

THIS IS ANOTHER way to get the best value from the cheaper cuts of venison – or indeed from a hare, rabbit or pheasant if you are lucky enough to have had rather a lot of either of them recently. If you want to bulk this dish out it can be served on your favourite pasta – mine is penne. One day I must try cooking this on top of a layer of pasta – perhaps even with some spinach under the pasta – but I cannot think what to put finally on top. Cheese sauce? But sometimes my wife and our carers suggest why not do something that we know works well.

450g/1lb venison, minced
1 medium onion (ideally red), finely chopped
50g/2oz fresh white breadcrumbs
1 tsp ground cumin
1 tsp ground coriander
1 fresh red chilli, deseeded and finely chopped
1 egg, beaten
Freshly ground black pepper
Handful of chopped coriander and flat parsley
Salt (optional)
2 tbsp olive oil

For the sauce:
1 tbsp olive oil
1 medium onion, finely chopped
400g/14oz can chopped tomatoes
500g/1lb 2oz carton passata (sieved tomatoes) or 4 tbsp tomato purée
300ml/10fl oz red wine
2 tsp hot pepper sauce (or a mixture of ½ tsp paprika and ¼ tsp chilli powder)
Salt and freshly ground black pepper

Preheat the oven to 180°C/350°F/Gas Mark 4. It is best to start with the sauce so that it can simmer away while you make the venison balls. Heat the oil in a casserole, or a stainless-steel pan with a good lid. Fry the onion until it is soft and golden. Add the chopped tomatoes, passata (or purée), red wine and pepper sauce. Try the taste and add salt and pepper as needed. Then leave it simmering on a low heat. If it threatens to dry out, add a little warm water.

For the meatballs, thoroughly mix in a bowl, the onion, minced venison (or other game), breadcrumbs, cumin, coriander, chilli, egg, a little freshly ground black pepper and the chopped parsley and coriander. I use very little salt but you may want to add a little at this stage. I prefer to combine ingredients like this by hand (even if the 'phone does always go when I am doing so) but you could use a processor – but it is easy to overdo it and lose the texture (and it is something to get out, wash up and put away). Anyway, you have to use your hand to form balls – no bigger than golf balls.

Heat the oil in a big frying pan and fry the balls in batches, if needs be, until they are nicely brown all over. Put them on to kitchen paper to take off any surplus oil, then place in a casserole with the sauce. Make sure the lid is firmly on, then put them in the oven for 40-45 minutes, by which time they should be cooked through and the sauce nicely thickened. Serve straight onto plates, over the pasta if you are using that.

Venison with fruit and spices

THIS RECIPE OWES something to the North African tagines, usually of chicken, lamb or goat. If you want to go overboard with the Moroccan connection, you could serve it with couscous. If you feel more north European – or even British – I think mashed or creamed potatoes go rather well. Venison has become expensive but you don't need the best cuts for this recipe. Shanks are ideal but it pays to sever the sinews so that the meat readily falls off the bone when cooked, so make some deep cuts down the length of the shanks. DM.

4 venison shanks
2 tsp salt
½ tsp freshly ground black pepper
2 tsp paprika
3 tbsp olive oil
2 medium onions, chopped
3 garlic cloves, chopped
Small handful of mint, chopped
½ tsp allspice
2 tsp ground coriander
1½ tsp ground ginger
2 tsp cumin
½ tsp ground cinnamon
600ml/1 pint beef stock
A good big glass of red wine
4 heaped tbsp tomato purée
225g/8oz carrots, sliced lengthwise
225g/8oz butternut squash flesh, diced
225g/8oz ready-to-eat dried apricots
Juice of 1 lemon
½ tsp cayenne pepper

Preheat the oven to 170°C/325°F/Gas Mark 3 and put a lidded Le Creuset casserole in to warm. Mix the salt, half of the black pepper and 1 tsp of the paprika in a small bowl and rub the mixture into the shanks and into the cuts. Heat half the oil in a heavy pan and brown the shanks. Remove and set aside in the warm casserole.

Add the remaining oil and cook the onions and garlic until golden and soft. Add half of the mint, the rest of the pepper and the paprika, the allspice, coriander, ginger, cumin and cinnamon and mix well into the onion and garlic. Add the stock, red wine and tomato purée, bring it all to the boil and pour over the venison.

Put the casserole into the oven for 2 to 2½ hours, then bring it out and stir in the carrots, butternut squash and apricots, then the lemon juice, the remainder of the mint and the cayenne pepper. Return to the oven for another 30 minutes or until the meat is falling from the bone and the vegetables are done.

Crusted loin of venison

LOIN OF HERB-crusted venison with smoked bacon, spring onions and sage mash, served with warm Cumberland sauce, is a recipe from Jeremy Ashpool of Jeremy's Restaurant, Borde Hill, near Haywards Heath in Sussex. It is one of my favourite restaurants. For convenience you could prepare the Cumberland sauce ahead, as it will keep beautifully for up to 2 weeks in the fridge. Jeremy also cooks a wonderful confit of duck, but you will have to go there to try that. Bookings on 01444 441102.

You will need a good game dealer or a friendly butcher to prepare a good piece of loin cut from the saddle for this quickly prepared dish. Even with minimal hanging, a nicely cooked piece of venison fillet will cut like butter. The secret is simply not to overcook it. A little wilted spinach would be an attractive additional vegetable to serve with the dish.

1 tsp chopped thyme
½ tsp chopped rosemary
Half a dozen or so juniper berries, crushed
550g/1lb 4oz venison loin, free of sinew and cut into 4 equal pieces
2-3 tbsp olive oil, for frying
Pinch or two of Maldon's sea salt

Freshly ground black pepper

For the mash potato:
450g/1lb King Edward potatoes, peeled and cut into regular-size pieces
4 rashers, unsmoked back bacon, chopped
6 sage leaves, chopped

*1 bunch of spring onions,
    chopped*
*Little freshly grated
    nutmeg*
*25-50g/1-2oz unsalted
    butter*
*Little single cream
    (optional)*
*Salt and freshly ground
    black pepper*

For the Cumberland sauce:
1 lemon, pared
1 orange, pared
*4 heaped tbsp good-quality
    redcurrant jelly*
4 tbsp port
1 heaped tsp Dijon mustard
1 tsp ginger, freshly grated
*A little cornflour for
    thickening*

First, prepare the Cumberland sauce. Blanch the thinly pared rind of the orange and lemon to remove bitterness. Stir the redcurrant jelly into the port over a gentle heat in a small saucepan. When melted, add the mustard, juice of the whole orange and half of the lemon (discard the remainder). Finally add the ginger and the rind. A little cornflower and water whisked in will give a coating consistency if you like a thicker sauce. Simmer for 10 minutes or so, then set aside. Whilst traditionally served cold, there is no reason why this great British sauce should not be served warm as an accompaniment to a hot dish.

Mix the seasoning of herbs and juniper, salt and pepper for the venison, coat the pieces lightly in the mixture and set them aside to take on the flavours.

Preheat the oven to 180°C/350°F/Gas Mark 4. Put the potatoes in a saucepan of water and boil as for normal mashed potatoes. Set aside (with a lid on top of the pan to keep the heat in) until the meat is resting for a few minutes after cooking.

The cooking of the venison could not be simpler. Heat the oil in your favourite frying pan until almost smoking hot and seal the pieces of meat on all sides. Remove from the hob and place the venison in a moderate oven for 6-8 minutes, depending on how rare you like your meat. Allow the meat to rest for a few minutes after cooking while you finish the potato dish, covering to keep warm. Gently fry the diced bacon in a heavy-based saucepan. Add the sage leaves and spring onions and stir together with a wooden spoon. Pass the potato through a potato ricer or mouli into a saucepan, adding the butter and a little cream, if you wish. Add the potato to the mixture in the saucepan and season to taste with salt, pepper and nutmeg.

Slice each piece of meat into three or four pieces and serve on plates warmed in the oven. Reheat the Cumberland sauce, unless serving cold. Either serve the vegetables and sauce separately or arrange on the plates in restaurant style.

Venison and lemon curry

THIS CURRY WAS inspired by a beef curry I had at my local Indian restaurant. The owner, Salam Ullah and his family are from Bangladesh. He is a wonderful chef and is always happy to talk about different recipes and ideas and often gives us unusual dishes to try.

I was curious about the flavours in the curry and wondered if the lemon was similar to the preserved lemons that I make for cooking my Moroccan tagines. It turned out to be something that I had never heard of.

The citrus fruit in this curry is Shatkora, from Bangladesh. It looks rather like a cross between a grapefruit, a lemon and a lime. It is really quite sour, but tenderizes the meat and gives a delicious tangy flavour. Shatkora is available in large Asian grocers or frozen in specialist food shops. DM.

450g/1lb stewing venison
    (or beef stewing steak),
    cubed
1 Shatkora, a quarter,
    chopped, or juice and
    zest of 1 lemon
300ml/10fl oz water
3 tbsp olive oil
1 onion, sliced
6 cloves garlic, grated

5 green chillies, thinly sliced
1 tsp ginger, grated
3 cardamom pods
3 cloves
1½ cinnamon sticks
1 tsp ground coriander
1 tsp ground cumin
1 tsp turmeric
1 tsp cayenne pepper
1 tsp garam masala

1 tsp paprika	Salt and freshly ground
1 tsp curry powder	black pepper
1 tbsp tomato purée	Fresh coriander,
1 tsp sugar	to garnish

Put the chopped Shatkora or lemon zest and juice into the water and set aside.

Preheat the oven to 180°C/350°F/Gas Mark 4.

Heat the oil over a medium heat, add the onion and cook gently until soft and lightly coloured.

Stir in the garlic, chillies, ginger, cardamom pods, cloves and cinnamon sticks. Cook carefully until the garlic just starts to brown. Add the remaining spices and tomato purée and stir until well mixed. Season with salt and pepper.

Pour in the water and Shatkora or lemon and simmer slowly until the mixture has thickened slightly. Stir in the cubed meat. Place in a lidded ovenproof casserole, and cook until the meat is tender. About 1½ hours. Check occasionally and add more water if necessary.

Sprinkle with some fresh chopped coriander and serve with basmati rice.

Venison and pasta bake

A REALLY EASY DISH full of rich flavours, and a great way to use up odd bits of venison. Serve with a green salad and a good glass of red wine. DM.

450g/1lb venison, minced
1 medium onion, coarsely
  chopped
2-3 cloves garlic, chopped
2 heaped tbsp tomato purée
25g/1oz plain flour
300ml /10fl oz beef stock
2 large beefsteak tomatoes,
  sliced
115g/4oz pasta twists or
shells (not penne, rather
  too large)
450g/1lb Greek low fat
  yogurt
2 eggs, beaten
Olive oil, for frying
Salt and freshly ground
  black pepper
Tiny bit of butter for
  greasing dish

Lightly grease an ovenproof dish and preheat oven to 190°C/375°F/Gas Mark 5.

Heat a couple of tablespoons of oil and gently fry the venison for about 5 minutes then add the onion and garlic. Keep stirring and cook for another 5 minutes.

Mix in the tomato purée and the flour and cook for a minute or so.

Pour in the stock and season to taste stirring well. Bring to the boil and simmer for 20 minutes.

Cook the pasta in slightly salted boiling water until al dente. Drain and set aside.

Put the meat venison mixture into the ovenproof dish and arrange a layer of tomatoes on the top.

Tip the pasta into a bowl and mix in the eggs and yogurt thoroughly. Spread over the top of the tomatoes and cook in the oven for about an hour.

Braised venison

Serves 6.

2.75kg/6lb haunch of
   venison
25g/1oz butter
1 tbsp olive oil
4 sticks celery, sliced
225g/8oz carrots, sliced
2 onions, sliced
1 bay leaf

1 tsp thyme, chopped
1 tsp chopped sage
¼ bottle red wine
300ml/10fl oz beef stock
25g/1oz butter
25g/1oz plain flour
1 tbsp cranberry jelly
Salt and black pepper

Preheat the oven to 190°C/375°F/Gas Mark 5. Trim the venison and melt the butter into the oil in a lidded casserole (I favour Le Creuset myself), then brown the venison all over.

Once it is nicely browned and sealed, which should take only a few minutes, remove it, preferably to a warm dish in the warming oven or on the plate warmer.

Then add the sliced celery, carrots, and onions and let them fry very gently for 5 minutes or so until they too are nicely browned.

Add the bay leaf, thyme and sage, then put the venison back on top of the vegetables and pour in the wine and enough stock to make sure it will not dry out. Do not overdo it; about a quarter of the way up the meat should be about right.

Make sure that the lid fits tightly and if needs be put a sheet of cooking foil under it and cook gently for 1½ hours.

Once it is cooked, slice the venison ready to serve and put it on a warm serving dish and return to a warm oven.

Warm a saucepan on a low heat, add the 1oz of butter, let it soften then add the flour a little at a time, mixing with a wooden spoon. Then gradually add the stock a little at a time, stirring it in until you have a smooth liquid. When that is all nicely hot add the cranberry sauce and pepper and salt to season.

Pour just a little over the sliced venison and put the rest into a sauce boat to take to the table.

That is it. Just present the sliced venison, the sauce and the cooked vegetables in a suitable dish to your guests.

Veni-burgers

I DO NOT OFTEN eat burgers of any kind, not only because the meat is often of poor quality, but so too are the buns. However burgers made from venison make a tasty variant of the rather dreary ones from the high street chains and nowadays the choice of freshly baked rolls at both Waitrose and my local M & S is very good. If you cannot find good rolls you can always serve the burgers as sandwiches.

As to the cheese, good quality Cheddar is ideal and, if like me, you need to watch your cholesterol levels, you will find some excellent goat cheddar with less side effects than statins. Makes 4 burgers.

4 bread rolls
350g/12oz coarsely chopped venison
1 large onion, finely chopped
1 tsp mixed chopped basil
and thyme
4 bun-sized 5mm/¼-inch thick slices Cheddar cheese
Salt and pepper
A little olive or rapeseed oil

Start by mixing the minced venison, chopped onion, herbs and seasoning.

Then divide the mixture into four portions and with a rolling pin flatten each into a bun-sized portion. Reserve those in the fridge for at least 90 minutes.

When you are ready for your snack, ideally during the lunch break on a cold winter's game shooting day, have the grill ready hot. Then fry the burgers in a pan with a little olive or rapeseed oil for about 5 minutes a side, put a slice of cheese on each one and brown under the grill.

Whilst that is going on, toast the buns. Serve the burgers piping hot on the toasted rolls with the apple quarters on the side.

*'Rabbit is good
food and good
sport'*

Rabbit

Oryctolagus cuniculus

The European rabbit

Season: All the year round

OUR RABBIT – the European rabbit – is one of seven different rabbits worldwide. The male is larger than the female. There seems to be some doubt about when it first came to these islands, with most accounts saying it was introduced from Africa and Iberia by the Normans. For some time they were encouraged to stay in warrens on farms or around manor houses, and were virtually farmed, but inevitably, being rabbits, they burrowed their way out and set up home in hedgerows and soft banks.

Rabbit was once an important part of the diet of country people and it was thought sufficiently valuable for landowners to use the law against poachers taking rabbits from their land. In more recent times, the war years excepted, it has come to be rather poorly regarded, especially the wild rabbit. Its proverbially prolific breeding ability led to its descent from a farmed animal to an agricultural pest, and the introduction of myxomatosis led to the sad sight of blind, disorientated rabbits infected with the disease staggering from roadside verges to a merciful death under the wheels of vehicles.

Despite all that, rabbit is good food – and good sport whether with the gun or ferrets and nets. Like most game it is best casseroled and for my money with mustard and cream in the French style. In general allow about 225g/8oz rabbit per head as a minimum, although I reckon four people can manage a whole skinned and cleaned rabbit of about 1.3kg/3lb.

There are those people who prefer cultivated to wild rabbits, and it is a source of endless amusement to me to read the views of those titans of the kitchen, Jane Grigson and her daughter Sophie. Grigson junior has no doubts: 'I'm not too keen on wild rabbits. I don't like the flavour as much and it is tough – I'd rather have domesticated rabbits any day.' Grigson senior is just as robust: '...good wild rabbit is a luxury. Domestic rabbit by contrast is as insipid as a battery chicken, even nasty in texture and taste.' Well, cooking is art more than science!

Rabbit terrine

PEOPLE DO NOT seem to make terrines at home very much these days, although they seem to be popular enough on restaurant menus. That is a pity, as they are not difficult. This recipe is simple enough, but it is best if eaten a couple of days after being made, so, if you intend to eat it on Sunday you will need to start to prepare it on Thursday. You will need a heavy terrine dish (the Le Creuset, of course) with a lid, or use an ovenproof baking dish of roughly the same dimensions – 32 x 10 x 10cm/ 12½ x 4 x 4in.

900g/2lb, or thereabouts, of boned rabbit
450g/1lb fat belly of pork, boned with the rind off
Fresh herbs – parsley (about a teaspoonful) and thyme – 3 sprigs
3 or 4 bay leaves
1 bottle of white wine (that is 600ml/1 pint for the recipe and the remaining 150ml/5fl oz for the cook)
225g/8oz streaky bacon rashers, half chopped and half in whole rashers
Salt and freshly ground black pepper

Place the rabbit and belly of pork in an earthenware dish, add the herbs and one of the bay leaves, a little salt and a lot of black pepper and cover with the wine. Cover with cling film (not kitchen foil) and leave to marinate overnight.

The following day, preheat the oven to 150°C/300°F/ Gas Mark 2. Take out the rabbit and pork but reserve the marinade. Mince the rabbit, the pork and the chopped bacon separately in a mincer, if you have one, or blitz it in a food processor. Put the meats into the terrine in alternate 1-2cm/½-¾in thick layers and cover with the bacon rashers. Use the remaining bay leaves as decoration. Pour in as much of the marinade as you can. Put on the lid and, if it is not a good fit, line with kitchen foil, but be sure to pierce it below the steam hole in the lid. Put in the oven for 3 hours, then remove and leave to cool slowly. Ideally, keep in the fridge for a couple of days before using.

Rabbit casserole

THIS RABBIT CASSEROLE/rabbit stew recipe is also the recipe for a rabbit pie filling (see page 174). As always you can work from the basic recipe below, which uses cider, or you can substitute dry white wine or beer. The choice of herbs – particularly the amounts you use – is simply a matter of what you like best. So try it this way first and then develop your own Lapin de la maison. Vegetables are a matter of choice. Jacket potatoes would go well with the casserole and your favourite winter root or green vegetable for both the casserole and the pie.

Plain flour, enough for covering the rabbit and a little for thickening the sauce
1 young rabbit, skinned and jointed
2 tbsp olive oil
1 medium onion, finely chopped
1 cooking apple, preferably Bramley, peeled, cored and diced
1 tsp chopped thyme

1 tsp freshly grated nutmeg, more if you like nutmeg, less if you are not keen on it
1 bay leaf
225g/8oz piece of streaky bacon (I prefer unsmoked), cut into 1cm/½in cubes
300ml/10fl oz dry cider
50g/2oz butter
Salt and freshly ground black pepper

Season a little of the flour with some salt and pepper and roll the jointed rabbit in it on a plate – or shake it all up in a plastic bag. Heat the olive oil in a deep stainless-steel pan with a lid. Gently fry the onion and apple, then remove with a slotted spoon to a plate. Sprinkle over the thyme and nutmeg and add the bay leaf.

Fry the rabbit and bacon in the remaining oil until lightly brown. Add the cider – bring it just up to the boil while scraping and incorporating all those sticky bits off the bottom of the pan, then immediately reduce to a simmer and tip the apple, onion, thyme, nutmeg and bay leaf into the pan. Season to taste then simmer for 1½-2 hours until the rabbit is tender.

In the meantime, gently warm and soften the butter in a saucepan and add the remaining 50g/2oz flour just a little at a time, stirring it with a wooden spoon to make a smooth, thick paste. Remove the meat with a slotted spoon and place it on a warmed serving dish (if you want to serve it smartly) or into a warmed container (if not). Let the stock bubble away while you add the butter and flour mix (or beurre manié if you are a Francophile) little by little, stirring with a wooden spoon to make a thickened sauce. For the smart dinner option, pour the sauce over the meat on the serving dish. Otherwise put the meat back in the pan and serve directly from that.

Rabbit pie

*450g/1lb shortcrust pastry
(homemade if you want
but chilled or thawed
frozen pastry is fine)*

*1 recipe quantity rabbit
casserole, thickened with
the beurre manié after
1½ hours of cooking (see
previous recipe)*

Roll out the pastry to a bit larger than the pie dish. Put
the dish upside down on the pastry and first cut a shape
about 2cm/¾in bigger than the dish all round. Then cut
the pastry to the size of the dish and remove the dish. You
now have the pie top plus a strip of pastry for the rim.

Put the thickened casserole mixture into the pie dish.
(I like to put a pie funnel in the dish to hold up the
middle of the pastry.) Dampen the rim of the dish and
press the strip of pastry that you cut on to the rim. Now
dampen that and the pastry lid and put that over the pie
and press down around the edge. The pie funnel will
make a steam hole in the middle of the pastry, but if
you're not using a funnel just cut a hole with a knife. If
you are not exhausted by now, you might try using some
of the leftover pastry to decorate the top of the pie – or
ask the children to cut it into flowers or bunnies to
decorate it. Put in the oven for 30 minutes or so to brown
the pastry.

Rabbit with saffron rice

THIS RECIPE IS based on one I found 50 years ago in a Penguin paperback *Plats du Jour*, which remains to this day my (recovered and rebound) bible on risotto. I include it because it is just that bit different – and the recipe for the saffron rice is really rather useful.

1 young rabbit, skinned and jointed
1 small onion
1 bay leaf
Juice of ½ lemon
1 celery stick, chopped
240-350ml/8-12fl oz Arborio rice
½ tsp saffron threads
2.5cm/1in piece of mace
2 cloves
2.5cm/1in piece of cinnamon stick or ½ tsp cinnamon powder
50g/2oz butter, plus a little extra for the rice
50g/2oz plain flour
½ bottle dry white wine
150ml/5fl oz single cream
½ tsp thyme
Salt and freshly ground black pepper

Put the rabbit, onion, bay leaf, lemon juice, celery, thyme and a little salt and pepper into a large stainless-steel saucepan and cover with water. Bring to the boil, then reduce to a gentle simmer for about 1½ hours or so to cook the meat until it can be stripped from the bones. Strain the stock and keep warm. Strip the meat and put in a warm oven on a serving dish covered with foil.

To cook the rice, use a large saucepan, not only to have enough water but to lessen the chance of it boiling all over the cooker. Bring to the boil. Add the rice, saffron, mace, cloves, cinnamon and a little salt. Bring the water back to the boil, give it all one good stir and reduce to a fairly fast simmer, it should be done in about 15-20 minutes but cooking time for rice varies so always read the instructions on the packet. Put a dish for the rice into the oven to warm.

In the meantime, melt the butter in a heavy-based saucepan and stir in the flour to form a smooth paste. Warm the wine gently in another pan and add to the paste a little at a time, stirring all the time to avoid lumps. Then stir in 300ml/10fl oz of the warm rabbit stock. As the rice is finishing, add the cream to the sauce, then keep it over a low heat. Drain the rice – add a dash of olive oil or a little butter – and put into the warm dish. When all is ready, pour the sauce over the rabbit and serve with the rice around it.

Rabbit with white wine and mushrooms

I LIKE COOKING WITH mushrooms – anything from sliced field mushrooms fried in olive oil and butter to go with calves liver and onions, to mushrooms in rich shin of beef and oxtail stews. They also go well with rabbit.

The choice of mushrooms is a matter of taste. I buy what looks good in Waitrose (except when I rustle up courage to pick the ceps in my garden). The chestnut mushrooms and portabellini are particularly good and the basic flat mushrooms are perfectly adequate, but I do not have much time for those little white jobs. Also, in this recipe you can perfectly well use dry cider rather than wine. Giving a precise cooking time for rabbit is not easy. The advantage of this dish is that it can be cooked during the day until it is almost done and finished off for the last half hour in time for dinner.

Serve the rabbit with a little parsley for decoration and croutons or with some mashed potato and seasonal vegetables.

Plain flour; enough to cover the joints, plus a little extra for thickening (optional)
1 young rabbit, jointed
1 tbsp olive oil

50g/2oz butter
225g/8oz piece of streaky bacon, cut into 1cm/½in cubes
2 medium onions, chopped
450g/1lb mushrooms, sliced

1 good big glass of dry
   white wine or cider
2 garlic cloves, finely
   chopped or crushed
1 bouquet garni
   (see page 18)
About 300ml/10fl oz lamb

stock (or better still
rabbit stock from the
bits and pieces) – use a
cube if you must
Salt and freshly ground
   black pepper
Parsley sprigs, to garnish

Preheat the oven to 170°C/325°F/Gas Mark 3. Season the flour with some salt and pepper and roll the rabbit joints in it on a plate – or shake it all up in a plastic bag. Heat the oil and butter in a large stainless-steel saucepan and brown the rabbit, bacon and onions gently. When the rabbit is browned on all sides and the onions golden and soft, add the mushrooms, the wine, the garlic, bouquet garni and stock. Let it all come just to the boil, then turn down to a fast simmer. Then, while it is bubbling, make sure to scrape all those lovely brown bits sticking to the pan (I have a favourite stainless-steel slice for this).

Then if the stainless-steel pan is suitable and has a lid, put it into the oven. If not, transfer the contents to a casserole. Either way, make sure the rabbit is just covered by the stock. Let it all simmer for about 2 hours or until the meat is tender. Towards the end of the cooking time, put a serving dish for the rabbit and plates into the oven to warm.

When the rabbit is cooked, remove it and the mushrooms, etc. to the serving dish and keep warm while you reduce the liquid by boiling until you have the right amount to pour over the rabbit. Of course, if you wish, you could thicken the sauce, instead of reducing, by stirring in a little flour (I always use a flour shaker for this to avoid getting lumps) or, better still, add bits of a beurre manié (see page 18) with a wooden spoon. Garnish with parsley and serve.

Rabbit with two mustards and cream

THIS IS A REALLY straightforward recipe – but it is my favourite way of eating rabbit. A decent-sized rabbit can be stretched to feed six people. It makes a generous meal for four, but remember that a wild rabbit is leaner and stronger-flavoured, and needs a little longer, slower cooking than a tame one. I think this goes well with mashed or creamed potatoes and celeriac and some steamed young carrots.

1 young rabbit, skinned and jointed into 6 pieces
Plain flour
2 tbsp olive oil
50g/2oz butter
115g/4oz piece of fat bacon, diced, or same weight of fat back rashers
4 large or 6 small shallots, chopped
1 bouquet garni (see page 18)

300ml/10fl oz game stock (see page 16) or chicken stock
150ml/5fl oz dry white wine
2 tbsp Dijon mustard
1 really heaped tsp dry English mustard powder
300ml/10fl oz double cream
Salt and freshly ground black pepper

Cut up the rabbit (or get the butcher to do it). This will give you the four legs, the rib cage and the saddle which is best cut into two portions (or even three). The floppy belly bits can be trimmed off and used for stock.

To do a really good job do not just get it skinned but take off the very thin under-skin, but do not spend too much time on that if in a hurry. It is a counsel of perfection.

Preheat the oven to 170°C/325°F/Gas Mark 3 (optional, see method below). Season the flour with some salt and pepper and roll the rabbit joints in it on a plate – or shake it all up in a plastic bag. Heat the olive oil and butter in a large stainless-steel saucepan and fry the rabbit pieces on all sides together with the bacon. Add the shallots, bouquet garni, stock and wine, bring briefly up to a fierce bubbling heat, then turn down to simmer, put on the lid and cook until the rabbit is tender – about 2-2½ hours. Alternatively, put the pan in the oven (or decant the contents into a casserole and put that in the oven) for the same time. Check during cooking to make sure it is not drying out. If needs be, add a little boiling water.

When the rabbit is done, remove it from the pan or casserole with a slotted spoon and keep warm. Spoon off any excess fat from the sauce. Thoroughly mix the two mustards into the cream, and add to the sauce in the casserole and warm through gently. Return the rabbit to the pan or casserole, make sure it is all thoroughly warmed through and serve.

Roast rabbit

I LOVED ROAST rabbit as a child during the wartime years'
(and post-war) rationing, but it seems rather unfashionable
these days. However, I cannot remember if my mother
stuffed the rabbit. In any event, you should make sure your
rabbit is not an old one. The best indicator of the age of a
rabbit is the ears: if young, they can be torn. Also the older
the rabbit, the tougher and more leathery his feet will look.
In any case, to be on the safe side, you should cook longer
at a lower temperature rather than trying a quick high-tem-
perature route. Lastly, I think that a forcemeat stuffing
helps to keep it all moist and avoids it drying out. Serve
with mashed potatoes and in winter roast parsnips or
mashed swede, and in summer broad beans.

1 young rabbit, cleaned,
    gutted and inner skin
    removed

For the meat stuffing:
115g/4oz bacon or ham,
    finely chopped
50g/2oz shredded suet
1 medium onion, chopped
Finely grated zest of
    ½ lemon

1 tsp chopped parsley
225g/8oz fat belly of pork
    or bacon rashers
1 tsp chopped thyme
2 eggs, well beaten
175g/6oz fresh white
    breadcrumbs
115g/4oz sausagemeat
Salt and freshly ground
    black pepper

Preheat the oven to 180°C/350°F/Gas Mark 4. Mix the chopped bacon or ham, the suet, onion, lemon zest and herbs in a bowl. Season well, add the breadcrumbs and sausagemeat, and blend them together. Then beat the eggs and blend them in too. Now stuff the rabbit with the forcemeat mixture. This can be quite a game depending on how the rabbit was butchered, and you will probably need a large needle, tough thread and more ability as a seamstress than I enjoy. Any stuffing that will not stay in the rabbit can be cooked later as forcemeat balls.

Wrap the pork rashers around the rabbit, using cocktail sticks to hold in place if necessary, put on a rack in a roasting tin and cook for 25-30 minutes per 450g/1lb total weight including the stuffing, with any surplus stuffing in balls under the rack.

Rabbit with prunes

Lapin aux pruneaux

I DISCOVERED FROM a Belgian friend that rabbit is enjoyed over there not least casseroled in white wine and, of course, with cream and mustard. But this recipe, given to me by Madame Micheline George-Maréchal, for rabbit with prunes is rather different. The meat marinates overnight so start this recipe the day before you want to eat it.

1 young rabbit, skinned and jointed
3 medium onions, sliced
1 carrot, sliced
1 celery stick, cut into chunks
2-3 thyme sprigs (dried if fresh is unavailable)
1-2 bay leaves
1 litre/1¾ pints brown ale or stout
2-3 tbsp white wine vinegar
1 garlic clove, sliced
175g/6oz smoked or unsmoked bacon, cut into lardons
50g/2oz lard or 3 tbsp sunflower oil
2 tbsp plain flour
25g/1oz sugar
12-15 prunes
Salt and freshly ground black pepper

Place the rabbit in an earthenware dish and cover with one of the sliced onions, the carrot, celery, garlic, thyme and bay leaves, together with the beer and vinegar. Cover with cling film (not kitchen foil) and leave to marinate overnight. The following day, strain the mixture through a colander, but reserve the marinade. Remove the carrot and celery and dry the pieces of rabbit on kitchen paper.

Heat a large stainless-steel saucepan and fry the bacon until slightly brown, then remove from the pan. Add the lard or oil and fry the remaining sliced onions until transparent, then place them with the bacon.

Adding a little more lard or oil if necessary, add the pieces of rabbit to the pan and sprinkle in the flour. Toss and turn the pieces until slightly golden. Add the previously cooked onions and bacon and pour the marinade (including the raw sliced onion) over the rabbit pieces. Add the prunes and sugar, and mix everything well before simmering gently with the lid on for about 1 hour until the rabbit is tender. Halfway through the cooking time, remove the prunes to a plate and take out the stones (unless already pitted). Squash the prunes with a fork and return them to the pan, then mix everything well for a delicious sauce. Season with salt and pepper to taste.

'Mad as a
march hare but
good to eat'

Hare

Lepus europaeus

Hare

OUR NATIVE HARE, the European Brown Hare *(Lepus europaeus)* is larger than the rabbit weighing some 3-4.5kg/7½-10lb. Living and nesting above ground on grassland, its prime defence is its sheer speed of 45 mph and remarkable manoeuvrability. The spring time boxing matches between hares, which probably gave rise to the expression 'mad as a March hare', were always thought to be between males competing for the favour of a female. Now it seems that the disputes are between over-amorous males and punch-slinging females not ready to mate.

There is an awful lot written about cooking hares, but I suspect that not many hares are eaten, and most people have never eaten it at all. This is partly because in most parts of the country hares were all but wiped out by modern intensive agricultural practice, but also because of the sheer attractiveness of the animal, its vulnerability as a ground-nesting creature, its courtship routines and its overwhelmingly sympathetic portrayal in literature and mythology. Strangely the hare (alongside the pig, the camel and badger) is one of the six mammals regarded as not kosher by practising Jews. There is also a certain mystique about cooking hare, not least the ritual use of the animal's blood and the mystery of jugged hare.

Well, it is an attractive creature, but so are many – particularly the wild ones – of the animals we eat. Fortunately, perhaps as a consequence of set aside, there has been an increase in the acreage of suitable habitat and certainly in parts of East Anglia hares are now increasing in numbers to the point of causing serious damage to cereal crops. Indeed I know of one 5,000-acre farm where over 300 hares are taken a year without any threat to their survival in healthy numbers. Fortunately for the hares that is a shooting estate so the population of foxes – their prime predator – is controlled.

As to the culinary mysteries of the hare – well, read on. As usual it is not so arcane as you may have been led to believe, but do watch out for that inner skin, or membrane. Like rabbits, hares have a second tightly fitting transparent skin, which should be removed before cooking. It is easy enough to peel away but if you do not do so it will rather spoil the dish.

Roast hare

WEIGHING IN AT 4.5kg/10lb, a hare is certainly big enough to roast, but usually the legs are reserved for casseroled dishes and it is only the saddle that is roasted. This can be something of a problem, since one saddle is enough for only two people. That is great if you are intent on an intimate meal with the one who means most to you, but not so good for the more usual meal for four people. It may be that your butcher will sell you two saddles or that a farming friend will let you have two whole hares. If not, here is a recipe for two using one saddle, but if you leave it attached to the rear legs you will have a meal for at least four (indeed up to six). In that case, simply double the ingredients for the sauce.

This will go well with my favourite creamed potatoes and celeriac. You might like to add a purée of chestnuts or a green vegetable such as broad beans or those very young Brussels sprouts. Elizabeth David suggests beetroot, cooked as usual, then chopped, reheated with butter and seasoning and a touch of vinegar. I have not tried this, but who am I to argue with that great lady? This will serve 2 (or 4-6 with the legs).

1 saddle of hare (or saddle plus 4 legs)
4 (or 8) streaky bacon or fat belly of pork rashers
1 tbsp brandy (optional)

150ml/5fl oz double or thick single cream
A small amount of hare stock if you have it, or use a lamb stock cube

A little plain flour, for
   thickening
1-2 tbsp port

1 tbsp redcurrant or rowan
   jelly

Preheat the oven to 220°C/425°F/Gas Mark 7 if you
are satisfied your hare is a young one. If in doubt, use
190°C/375°F/Gas Mark 5. Put the hare on a rack in a
roasting tin and cover completely with the bacon. Roast
at 220°C/425°F/Gas Mark 7 for 20 minutes for a young
hare (the meat will be pink) or at 190°C/375°F/Gas Mark
5 for 30 minutes for an older one. Obviously, in both
cases, if it is a larger piece (i.e. with the legs on) it will
take longer – say another 10-15 minutes. Towards the end
of the cooking time, put a serving dish into the warming
oven or hot water.

When the hare is done, remove it from the oven and
transfer to the serving dish. Carve the saddle lengthwise
into strips of fillet. If you have cooked the legs too,
remove these and cut into legs and thighs. If you want to
make this a special dish, you might follow the way roast
hare was served at The Carved Angel and flambé the
hare with the brandy. In any case, lay the meat on the
warm serving dish with the crisp bacon and keep warm
in the warming oven or open your main oven door wide
and put it there.

Check the juices left in the roasting tin. If there is a lot
of fat, pour a little off, then add the cream, a little stock if
it seems short of liquid, a sprinkling of flour from a flour
shaker, the port and the redcurrant jelly to help it all
thicken. Season with salt and pepper. Bring all this up to
the boil in the roasting tin on the hob, stirring well with a

wooden spoon, then reduce the heat to a fast bubble and stir to dissolve the jelly (use a bit more if needed to thicken) while scraping up the bits stuck to the bottom of the roasting tin. Once it has thickened, pour the sauce over the hare and bacon and serve.

Jugged hare

THERE ARE ARGUMENTS over how the rich stew gained the name Jugged Hare, but it is most likely because it was often cooked in a tall earthenware pot – more the shape of a jug than a casserole. This could be covered and stood in a pan of bubbling water over a fire to ensure the hare would be cooked slowly. Of course some would argue that if the blood of the animal is used in the cooking, it then becomes a civet of hare. I leave this distinction aside but I still remember the joy of my brothers and I when through some miracle of backdoor dealings, usually by my grandfather, in the dark wartime years when there was not much to eat, our mother would announce that she had obtained a hare. Seventy years on in these days of plenty, the memory of jugged hare lives with me still. My mother served her jugged hare with mashed potatoes and swede – or even cabbage. I like some forcemeat balls as well. (There is an alternative – perhaps more exciting – recipe for forcemeat stuffing on page 182, which can be used for the forcemeat balls.)

Plain flour, enough to cover the joints, plus a little extra for thickening
1 hare, skinned and jointed
The liver, blood and brains of the hare (optional)
115g/4oz butter, plus extra for thickening (optional)
225g/8oz piece of streaky bacon, cut into 1cm/½in cubes
2 red onions, chopped
1 bouquet garni (see page 18)

Lots of chopped thyme (or 1
tsp dried thyme)
1 tbsp chopped parsley
300ml/10fl oz red wine – or
glass of port
Hare or beef stock as
needed (optional)
1 tbsp redcurrant jelly
Salt and freshly ground
black pepper

For the forcemeat balls:
115g/4oz fresh white
breadcrumbs
50g/2oz shredded suet
Lots of chopped thyme
1 tbsp chopped parsley
1 egg, beaten
Zest of 1 lemon, grated
50g/2oz ham or bacon,
chopped
25g/1oz butter, lard
or – best of all – goose
fat
Salt and freshly ground
black pepper

Preheat the oven to 150°C/300°F/Gas Mark 2. Season the flour with some salt and pepper and roll the hare joints in it on a plate – or shake it all up in a plastic bag. Melt the butter in a stainless-steel pan and brown the hare pieces and bacon. Transfer to a lidded Le Creuset casserole. Lightly fry the onions in the remaining fat, then add the herbs, meat, red wine and some stock. Bring up to the boil then transfer to the casserole. Add sufficient beef stock, if needed, to cover the meat.

Stand the casserole in a large pan or roasting tin of hot water and put into the oven. This should be cooked – tender enough for the meat to fall off the bone – in about 3 hours. When the meat is cooked, ladle some of the juices from the casserole. You can thicken this sauce by sprinkling in some flour from a flour shaker and stirring that in with the redcurrant jelly and a little butter (or cream if you have any spare in the fridge) with a wooden spoon until it comes to a simmer. Alternatively, you can mash the brains and liver with the blood and add this to the pan to thicken it. Do not let it boil. Blood boiling is not recommended anywhere (although these days mine often does) and certainly not in the kitchen. In either case, once the sauce has thickened, return it to the pot and keep warm while you make the forcemeat balls.

Mix all the ingredients for the forcemeat balls except for the fat or oil in a bowl. Form the mixture into small-ish balls (about 2.5cm/1in in diameter). Melt the butter, lard or goose fat (or heat the oil) in a stainless-steel frying pan and fry the balls until golden brown. Serve the hare from the pot into good wide soup bowls, accompanied by the forcemeat balls.

Mixed Game

Game pâté

YOU CAN MAKE a good pâté from a great variety of ingredients, but the basis has to be in the balance of the essential ingredients and the technique of cooking. Provided you get these right almost everything else is a matter of what is in the fridge and personal taste for garlic, herbs and texture. By processing some ingredients, such as the liver, hard pork fat and half the game meat less than others, the pâté can have an interesting texture.

The liver should be from any feathered or furred game – or pig's liver or, as a last resort, even supermarket chicken liver. Similarly, the meat should be from any feathered or furred game, with venison as an alternative.

More or less the same ingredients can be used for a game pie but (especially if it is to be served cold) then you should make a jelly of pig's trotters, the carcass of the birds and perhaps a knuckle of veal.

This recipe is for a good basic pâté. Once you discover how easy it is, then you should experiment to adjust the recipe to suit your own taste. In other words create your own pâté maison.

Ideally you should cook the pâté in a heavy Le Creuset terrine dish with a lid, or two smaller ones, but if you do not have the Le Creuset use a Pyrex dish but the deeper, narrower terrine dish is better.

115g/4oz liver
115g/4oz hard pork fat
225g/8oz game meat, from furred or feathered game, or venison
50g/2oz butter
1 medium onion, chopped
1 garlic clove, crushed – I use 2 good-sized cloves but you might prefer to use less
About 50g/2oz veal or steak (oddments of pie veal or off cuts of fillet steak are ideal)
2-3 bacon rashers
225g/8oz piece of fat belly of pork
6 black peppercorns, crushed
6 juniper berries

Breadcrumbs. Not too fine. I prefer fairly fresh white bread (proper bread not the ghastly wrapped plastic stuff). A good thick slice roughly crumbled by hand is best.
1 heaped tsp chopped thyme
2 heaped tsp chopped parsley
1 egg
Slug of brandy, Calvados or even port
Salt and freshly ground black pepper

To decorate:
1-2 bay leaves (optional)
2 glacé cherries, halved (optional)

Preheat the oven to 180°C/350°F/Gas Mark 4. You will want a mixture of textures in the pâté so put aside the liver, hard pork fat and half the game meat. Melt the butter in a stainless-steel frying pan and gently fry the onion and garlic just until they are soft and golden. Meanwhile, coarsely chop the veal or steak, bacon, belly of pork and half the game meat, then mince it quite finely in a food processor together with the crushed pepper-corns and juniper berries. Put the mixture in a bowl with the breadcrumbs and herbs and add the fried onion and garlic. Beat the egg and brandy and add that, season with salt and pepper, then gently mix by hand.

Now chop the liver, the hard pork fat and the rest of the game meat, which you've set aside, fairly small – about 5mm/¼in bits. Add all this to the other ingredients in the bowl and mix it all up. Use a wooden spoon and your hands to get a good even mixture. Put the mixture into the terrine dish or dishes, packing it in quite firmly. For decoration you can put a bay leaf or two or a couple of halved glacé cherries on top.

Pour a kettle of boiling water into a stainless-steel roasting dish, stand the terrine in the water and cook for about 1¼ hours with the lid on the terrine or a cover of extra thick (or doubled) kitchen foil over the Pyrex. You will know when it is cooked because the fat coming out will be clear in the dish with the pâté floating on it. If in doubt, test with a skewer, which should come out clean. To make it look really good, take off the lid or foil for the last 10 minutes so that the top of the pâté browns.

The pâté will be improved if you gently press it as it cools by putting weights on top. Replace the foil (if you removed it) first, then put cans of tomatoes or bags of pasta or lentils on top – they all seem to work quite well.

Game pots

GAME POTS MAKE an interesting alternative to making a pâté, using much the same ingredients of mixed game. This is another recipe from my illustrator, Debby Mason, who can cook as well as paint and draw.

550g/1lb 4oz mixed game meat (pheasant, roast pigeon and a little venison work well)
4 cloves
¼ tsp ground mace
4-5 tbsp Madeira
115g/4oz butter, plus extra for greasing
1 tbsp stock, either bird or rabbit
Salt and freshly ground black pepper

Put the meat pieces in a large stainless-steel saucepan with the cloves, mace and a little salt. Just cover with cold water and bring to the boil, then turn the heat down and, with the lid on, simmer very slowly for about 2 hours until the meat is tender. Remove the meat (allowing the liquid to drain back into the pan) and chop finely in a food processor.

Reduce by about two-thirds then stir in 4 tbsp of the Madeira and half of the butter with a wooden spoon. Once the butter has melted into the liquid, add the minced meat and stir to make a smooth pâté. If the mixture is too thick, add a little more Madeira or a spoonful of stock. Season to taste with salt.

Spoon the mixture into buttered ramekin dishes. Melt the remaining butter in a small saucepan and pour a little over the contents of each ramekin to seal. Chill in the fridge and serve as a starter with crispy French bread (you can buy pretty good baguettes ready to cook from good supermarkets) and a little green salad. I like rocket and watercress.

Mixed game pie

THIS IS ANOTHER of those end of season recipes to use up the bits and pieces which have accumulated in the freezer, although it is very good at any time. The first time I experimented with it I made the foolish mistake of mixing venison with pheasant and pigeon and partridge. However we all learn from our mistakes and I now use either a mixture of quicker cooking meats such as pheasant, pigeon and partridge or a slow cooking mixture of venison, hare and rabbit.

The marinade is suitable for either mix. Remember that the meats need to be in the marinade for about twenty-four hours before you start cooking.

As to vegetables, that is very much a matter of personal preference but in the depth of winter there are few nicer things than mashed buttered swedes and broad beans.

Serves 6.

The meat of a pheasant and
a partridge
3 or 4 pigeon breasts
1 apple
2 shallots
½ tsp chopped thyme
2 tbsp red wine or port
2 tbsp quince jelly
Large packet shortcrust
pastry

For the marinade:
1 clove garlic, chopped
2 shallots, chopped
1 small carrot, chopped
1 stick celery, chopped
Skin and bones of the birds
6 juniper berries
Herbs to taste
Pepper and salt
Large glass red wine

Put the chopped meats into the marinade for 24 hours.

Then cook them gently on the top of the stove in something like my favourite big heavy-lidded, stainless-steel casserole, together with the apple cut into eight portions, the two shallots quartered and the half teaspoon of chopped thyme, until the meat is tender. That should be about 30 to 35 minutes.

Once that is done drain the meat well, stir in the port and quince jelly and put aside.

Preheat the oven to 200°C/400°F/Gas Mark 6.

Here you come to a choice. You can go for the sensible option using an ordinary Pyrex pie dish, or the adventurous one using a pudding basin large enough to take all the ingredients. The trouble with the latter is that you will run the risk of the whole thing collapsing when you turn it out onto a serving dish!

Either way you will need to lightly grease the container with soft butter and line it with pastry. Then put the meat etc. into that, turning over the pastry to cover it all neatly, and cutting away any surplus. Brush the exposed pastry with a little milk to help it brown and put it in the oven to bake for 30-40 minutes, or until the pastry is golden brown.

Once all is ready, including the vegetables, get everyone seated and serve the pie at the table. If you have taken the tricky option with the pudding basin and it all collapses when you turn it out, just smile and refill the glasses.

*'Good for the table,
good for the heart'*

Salmon

Salmonidae family

Salmon

STRICTLY SPEAKING salmon is not game, but it is a game fish and until the advent of farmed salmon all salmon was hunted and caught in the wild. Nowadays I am told there are eighty times as many farmed salmon as wild ones in the world, although how anyone can know that puzzles me.

As we all learned at school salmon are anadromous, that is they hatch in fresh water, make their way to the sea and return to fresh water spawning grounds to mate, lay their eggs and mostly then to die. I was taught that salmon return to the very spot where they hatched to spawn but nowadays there seems some doubt about that.

Sadly there seems little doubt about the effects of salmon farming upon the wild salmon population. It is devastating, and the Atlantic wild salmon is now in serious decline. In Alaska farming is prohibited and so far the Pacific stock seems to be in good shape.

The problem seems to stem from both the high density of fish per cubic metre of water and the feeding techniques used. The large amounts of uneaten food accumulating on the sea floor of the salmon pens and the density of population give rise to disease and leave the fish vulnerable to sea lice which are transmitted to the wild population by escaping fish. It is the sort of man–made problem for which Prince Charles is often derided for warning us about.

Farmed salmon is different to the wild fish because of its different diet and it is said to have less of the Omega 3 fatty acids which they (whoever 'they' are) say are good for us. According to some reports it may have more of those nasty dioxins and farmed salmon are fed red colouring material whereas the wild salmon obtains its colourant naturally in its diet. Despite all this the American Medical Association concluded nearly twenty years ago that eating farmed salmon is on balance good for us – but, of course, true wild salmon is much better.

They (it is them again) say, and so does my wife, that I should not eat meat every day, so to help with meatless days here are three excellent ways to cook salmon.

Salmon in pastry

I FIRST ATE SALMON in this style more than thirty years
ago at the Connaught Grill when I was the Minister for
Shipping at a meeting with Y.K. Pao, the Hong Kong
shipping magnate. It was so good that I did not rest until
I had ferreted out the recipe, and my wife and I cooked it
together for ourselves. Some years later I found a very
similar recipe in Jane Grigson's *English Food* published in
1974. I suppose it would not be politically correct to use
that title these days!

This recipe sounds a bit difficult but really it isn't
though you do need to stick to the cooking instructions.
Of course you may like to use more ginger or almonds –
that is a matter of taste – but I think this way of cooking
salmon is an absolute winner. If there is any left over, it is
very good cold.

Coordination is needed to get the salmon and sauce
ready at the same time. Do not make the sauce too early
or cook it for too long or you may find that it will separate. It will still taste just as good but it looks a bit
uninviting. If you have two ovens, you can make the sauce
ahead of time and place it in the second oven to keep
warm, along with the plates. If you do not have two ovens,
start to make the sauce about 10 minutes after the
salmon has gone into the oven. Alternatively, if you are
preparing this for guests and do not want to be in the
kitchen while everyone else is chatting (and drinking),
you can prepare the sauce up to cooking the shallots etc.,

then put it on one side to reheat and add the cream and mustard just before the salmon parcel is cooked. This recipe serves 6.

900g/2lb salmon fillet from the tail end, skinned and cut into 2 matching pieces
115g/4oz butter, at room temperature
1 tbsp raisins
1 tbsp blanched almonds, chopped
4 pieces preserved ginger in syrup, chopped
Flour, for dusting
350g/12oz shortcrust pastry (homemade if you want, but chilled or thawed frozen pastry is fine)
1 egg, beaten

For the sauce:
85g/3oz butter
3 shallots, chopped
1 tsp chopped parsley
1 tsp chopped tarragon
1 tsp chopped chervil
1-2 tbsp plain flour
2 tsp Dijon mustard
450ml/16fl oz thick single cream (or ordinary single if not available)
3 egg yolks
1 tsp lemon juice (optional)
Salt and freshly ground black pepper

Preheat the oven to 220°C/425°F/Gas Mark 7. Soften the butter in a mixing bowl by beating it a little with a wooden spoon, then stir into it the raisins, chopped almonds and chopped pieces of ginger to make a paste. This is to stick the two pieces of salmon together, one on top of the other, and to go on the outside of the resultant salmon sandwich.

Now for what I find is the tricky bit. On a work surface lightly dusted with flour, roll the pastry out sufficiently to make an envelope for the salmon. That is, it needs to be more than twice the area of the fish. Once it is rolled out, lay it over a baking tray with a slightly raised rim and place one of the fish pieces in the middle of it. Cover the fish with half the paste, place the other piece of fish on top and use the rest of the paste to coat the outside of the salmon sandwich.

Now fold the pastry over to encase the salmon completely. The pastry will stick together best if you just dampen (with finger or pastry brush) one side of the join and press it together really tightly. Close the ends in the same way, then cut a few slashes through the top of the pastry to let out the steam when it is cooking. Thin the beaten egg with 1 tsp of water, if you like, and paint it over the pastry to form a glaze. If you feel artistic (or if the children do), any spare bits of pastry could be used to decorate the envelope. They will stick to the glaze, but make sure to glaze them in turn. Put the salmon in the oven for about 30 minutes. Once the pastry is done, so will be the fish.

To make the sauce, start by very, very gently frying the chopped shallots and herbs in the butter. I use a small saucepan rather than a frying pan. Do not let it brown, you are really stewing the shallots rather than frying them. Once they are soft, stir in the flour – something between one and two dessertspoons. You will know when it is enough as it will form a shallot, butter and flour paste with neither any butter nor flour not absorbed. Then gently add the mustard and the cream (except to save 3 tablespoons to mix with the egg yolks) all the time over a low heat and let it cook for 10 minutes or so. Now beat up the egg yolks and the cream you saved and stir it into the sauce – still over a low heat. Do not let it boil – just cook it gently and it will thicken. Add pepper and salt to taste. You may like to sharpen it with a little lemon juice but that is a matter of taste.

Warm a serving dish and sauceboat. Slide the parcel of salmon carefully on to the warm dish without breaking it. Pour the sauce into the warm sauceboat and let everyone help themselves.

Salmon coulibiac

IN SOME WAYS this is a method of feeding the same number of people as in my Salmon in Pastry recipe, but with half as much salmon. In another way it is a fish pie that is even more up market than my favourite one, the Two Fat Ladies' wonderful recipe. As ever, a good fish pie takes a bit of effort, but it is worth it. A coulibiac is a mixture of fish, rice, herbs, onions, eggs and mushrooms, baked in pastry. If you want to avoid pastry, you could cook it in a pie dish with a breadcrumb (just dotted with butter) topping.

I really cannot think of anything to go with this other than a really good fresh mixed green salad. The great Delia Smith suggests foaming Hollandaise sauce. Well, you can if you like, but by the time I have cooked the coulibiac I have had enough of the kitchen and want to get my feet under the table. Of course, these days Delia might say to buy your Hollandaise at Waitrose, and I think that is good advice. Serves 6.

680g/1½lb salmon fillet
A few peppercorns
1 bouquet garni (see page 18)
85g/3oz basmati or
   American long grain rice
600ml/1 pint fish stock – or
   more – see below
   (optional)

2 pinches of turmeric
85g/3oz butter
1 medium onion,
   chopped
175g/6oz mushrooms (you
   can use button, chestnut
   or shiitake – but not flat
   ones), chopped

*1 heaped tbsp chopped dill
or 1 tsp good freeze-
dried dill*
*1 heaped tbsp chopped
parsley*
2 hard-boiled eggs, chopped
*450g/1lb puff or shortcrust
pastry (homemade if*
*you want, but chilled or
thawed frozen pastry is
perfectly all right)*
1 egg, well beaten
*Salt and freshly ground
black pepper*

Preheat the oven to 220°C/425°F/Gas Mark 7. Put on the eggs to hard boil. First you need to partly cook the salmon. You could bake it for 10 minutes in buttered kitchen foil, but, as for all fish pies, I think it best to poach it in a big shallow pan until it is ready to flake. Do not overdo it. You could use just plain water or the fish stock with the peppercorns and bouquet garni, but half and half water and white wine will certainly improve it.

While that is going on, cook the rice. Rice (even good basmati) is so variable that I simply follow the instructions on the bag, but adding turmeric to give flavour and colour. Do not overcook – you want it just al dente. (Alternatively, treat it more like a risotto. That is, melt 15g/½oz of butter in a saucepan, fry the rice in it until all the butter is absorbed, then add either hot water or fish stock and the turmeric, a little at a time as it is absorbed, until the rice is swollen up and, again, just al dente.)

Melt 85g/3oz butter in a large stainless-steel pan and very gently fry the onion. As it softens, add the chopped mushrooms and keep cooking gently until it is all nicely soft, adding the herbs towards the end. Now put this onion and mushroom mixture, the rice, the flaked salmon and the chopped hard-boiled eggs into a bowl and mix it well with plenty of pepper and a little salt.

The objective now is to encase a sausage shape of this mixture in the pastry. Roll out the pastry sufficiently to cover the salmon and rice mixture. Lay it over a lightly oiled or buttered baking tray with a shallow rim and lay the salmon and rice mixture in layers to form a loaf or cake shape on it. Fold the pastry over and seal by dampening one side and pressing it hard on the other to make a seam and tuck in the ends in the same way. Glaze it all with the well-beaten egg (to which my wife says add a tiny drop of water).

As ever, if you have any bits of pastry left, you might use it for decoration. I am not much good at this, but young children seem to have the knack of it. Cook for 25 minutes, but keep an eye on it to make sure the pastry is cooked but not overcooked.

Simple salmon

ALL THIS NEEDS is a fillet of salmon, a Le Creuset skillet and a little olive oil. Pour a little oil on to a plate and turn the salmon in it. Brush the skillet with a little oil and heat until it begins to smoke.

Put the salmon in the skillet, skin-side down first (it is easier to turn it over that way). Depending on the thickness of the fillet, give it about 5 minutes to char or sear the skin. Then with a large stainless-steel slice (the plastic ones are not sharp or rigid enough) under it and another on top, turn it over and cook on until it is seared on the outside but not dry or overcooked.

Serve with a green salad or, if in season, green beans or mangetout.

*'When Debby wants scallops
for dinner, she simply dives
for them'*

Scallops,
Spider crabs,
Mackerel

Pectinidae family, Maja squinado,
Scombridae family

Scallops, spider crabs
and mackerel, 220

Simple barbecued scallops
with bacon, 222

Scallops with figs,
Parma ham and St. Agur, 224

Spider crab spaghetti with chilli,
tiger prawns and asparagus, 226

Roasted garlicky crab claws, 228

Barbecued mackerel with pesto, 230

Mackerel cooked in seawater, 232

Scallops, spider crabs and mackerel

Season (UK): Fresh diver-caught scallops in their shells should be avoided between May and August as this is when they spawn. For spider crabs, late summer and autumn

THESE RECIPES ARE by Debby Mason, my illustrator. Debby is a keen scuba diver and fisherman (not, I am glad to say, a fisherperson), and when she wants scallops for dinner she simply dives for them, whilst most of us have to head for the fishmongers or supermarket.

I know that I am stretching the definition of game to include scallops, but they are just too good to leave out. Diver-caught scallops are a must, as they are environmentally sound and each one hand-picked. Trawler-dredged scallops tend to be tiny in comparison and the damage caused by the trawler's bottom gear ripping through the seabed not only causes severe damage to the scallops' breeding ground but also decimates the whole flora and fauna of the seabed, which can take decades to recover.

In Europe, spider crabs are a delicacy and very expensive, mainly because many are imported from the UK where the majority of us impatient Brits cannot be bothered to extract the meat. However they are definitely worth persevering with, as the meat is sweet and full of flavour.

Debby was trying to find a spider crab to draw, and approached her local 'trade' fish market. Unfortunately she was told that they could only supply them by the tonne! A chance encounter in the pub with a local fisherman secured half a dozen beautiful spider crabs, one of which she drew, the rest inspired the recipe on page 226.

Simple barbecued scallops with bacon

No MATTER WHAT famous chefs may say, in my experience if a scallop is fresh then it will not turn to rubber if overcooked. This makes them ideal for a barbecue, but good results can also be achieved by grilling. Serve with fresh crusty bread. DM.

4 rashers of streaky bacon,
    cut into short strips,
    or lardons
1 medium onion or
    4 shallots, finely diced
2-3 garlic cloves, crushed
Half a stick of celery
    (remove stringy bits),
    finely chopped
1 tbsp chopped parsley

8 fresh whole diver-caught
    scallops in their shells
2-3 tbsp olive oil
25g/1oz butter
300ml/10fl oz single cream
    or crème fraîche
Freshly ground black
    pepper
4 tbsp brandy or Noilly
    Prat (optional)

Heat 1 tbsp of olive oil in a stainless-steel frying pan and fry the bacon over a high heat for a minute or two to brown and then reduce the heat and add the onions and garlic. Cook further until the onions just start to go translucent, then stir in half the parsley and remove from the heat.

Open the shells and remove the muscle and coral, keeping the cleaned shells to one side. Cut the scallop muscle across the middle, creating two discs, then cut each disc in half. If you like the orange coral, then also cut these in half and remove the tube running through the middle. (Some people prefer not to eat the orange coral, so this is optional depending on your taste.)

Add a little of the remaining oil, to stop them sticking, and a knob of butter to each of the deeper half of the scallop shell. Add the muscle and coral (if using) and place under a preheated hot grill or on a rack over a hot barbecue. When the scallop and the butter start to brown, add the bacon, celery and onion mixture to each scallop shell and also add 2 tbsp cream or crème fraîche. At this stage, as an option, you might like to add a dash of brandy or Noilly Prat. Continue to cook until the mixture starts to bubble and brown. Top with black pepper and the remaining chopped parsley and serve immediately.

Scallops with figs, Parma ham and St. Agur

THIS STARTER IS a dish that St. Agur (whoever he was) would have died for. DM.

Serves 2.

2 large ripe figs
8 fresh diver-caught
    scallops, white muscle
    only
25g/1oz St. Agur cheese
4 slices of Parma ham
2 tbsp Parmesan cheese,
    grated

2 tbsp balsamic vinegar
Some olive oil for frying
    and drizzling
Cornflour, to dust
50g/2oz butter
Freshly ground black
    pepper

Preheat the oven to 180°C/350°F/Gas Mark 4. Cut the figs from the stalk end, halfway down. Turn through 90 degrees and make another cut down at right angles to the first to form a cross. Then open the figs gently so they look rather like lilies. Cut the St. Agur in half and put one half in each of the figs and then carefully close them to look like whole figs again. Then, for each fig lay two slices of the ham in a cross shape, put the fig in the middle and use the ham to make it into a parcel (a cocktail stick can help to hold it together).

Put the figs on a baking tray (preferably a non-stick-coated one), sprinkle with the grated Parmesan and drizzle with the balsamic vinegar and a little of the olive oil. Bake for 10 minutes. Do not overdo it: the cooking seems to enhance the St. Agur to the point where it can simply overpower the delicate flavour of the fig.

While that is going on, dust the scallops with a little cornflour, heat the remaining olive oil and the butter in a stainless-steel frying pan and gently fry the scallops until brown on one side and then flip over to brown the other.

Serve with the figs (and a simple green salad), adding a little more Parmesan, black pepper and balsamic vinegar.

Spider crab spaghetti with chilli, tiger prawns and asparagus

THE ASPARAGUS IN this dish is used to add a splash of colour and to diffuse the chilli. It is interesting that in this dish the different flavour combinations keep changing right through to the last mouthful. Serve with an over-chilled crisp white wine. DM.

115g/4oz butter
2 tbsp olive oil
2 red chillies (10cm/4in each), deseeded and sliced across the width
2-3 garlic cloves, crushed
10-12 fresh baby asparagus spears, cut into 2.5cm/1in lengths
500g/1lb 2oz fresh spaghetti or linguine
12 raw tiger prawns
280g/10oz cooked spider crab leg meat or white crab meat
Juice of 1 lemon or lime
1 tbsp chilli oil
White truffle oil (optional)
Salt and freshly ground black pepper

Warm the butter in a small saucepan until a darkish, nutty brown (beurre noisette), skim off the froth and add the olive oil and return to the heat. When the butter mixture is hot, add the chillies and garlic and heat for a minute or so to allow the chilli and garlic to infuse.

Remove from the heat and set aside. Cook the fresh pasta in boiling salted water for 3 minutes or as instructed. Steam the asparagus for a few minutes over boiling water.

(Asparagus cooks very quickly, so ensure that you remove it from the heat while it still has some bite to it.)

When the pasta is nearly al dente, reheat the chilli and garlic butter and add the prawns. As soon as they have turned pinkish, add the asparagus and the cooked spider crabmeat and heat through gently, then season with a little salt and pepper and a good squeeze of lemon juice.

Drain the pasta (leaving a little water still clinging to it) and stir in the chilli oil, then mix in all the remaining ingredients and season to taste with salt and pepper. Serve immediately on hot plates, drizzled with the white truffle oil (if using) and finished with freshly ground black pepper.

Roasted garlicky crab claws

RATHER MESSY TO eat, but with fresh French bread to soak up the slightly caramelised and very yummy garlic juices well worth the picking. DM.

4 medium-sized cooked
  brown crab claws
75g/3oz salted butter
Splash of olive oil
4 garlic cloves, peeled and
  finely chopped or crushed
2 garlic cloves, whole and
  unpeeled

3 sprigs fresh thyme, lightly
  crushed
1 lemon
Handful fresh parsley,
  chopped
Freshly ground black
  pepper

Preheat the oven to 200°C/400°F/Gas Mark 6. Very carefully, give each section of the crab claws a hefty whack with the back of a heavy knife to crack the shells to make them easier to pick and let the juices soak in.

Gently heat the butter and a splash of olive oil in a large saucepan then add all the garlic and the thyme. Be careful not to let it burn. Once the garlic has softened add the crab claws and spoon the melted butter all over them. When hot, tip the claws, half the parsley, the juice of half a lemon, black pepper and buttery juices into a roasting dish and put in the oven for 5-10 minutes, remove once the claws are heated through and the juices are lightly browned.

Sprinkle with the remaining parsley. Serve with quarters of the remaining lemon.

Have plenty of French bread to soak up the juices.

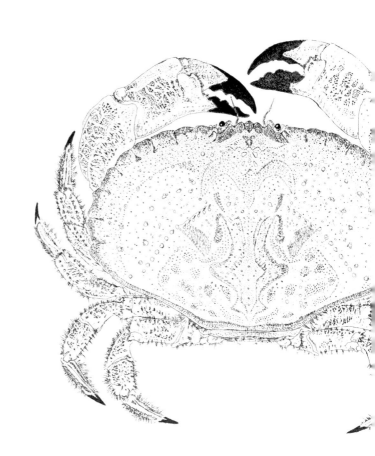

Barbecued mackerel with pesto

THIS IS A WONDERFUL dish which is perfect if you are on holiday and go on a mackerel fishing trip. Unless the fish really are not biting, you should leave with plenty for supper. DM.

Mackerel, fresh and filleted but leave the skin on

For the pesto (If you have a food processor, brilliant, if not and you are camping, a long shot but you will need a pestle and mortar. Or, a jar of ready-made pesto sauce which is just as good):
25g/ 1oz basil leaves, stalks removed
3 cloves garlic, peeled
5 tbsp grated Parmesan
3 tbsp pine nuts
5 tbsp olive oil
Salt and freshly ground black pepper

Mix the basil, garlic, Parmesan and pine nuts together, either in a food processor or grind up with a pestle and mortar. Season to taste with salt and freshly ground black pepper. Slowly add the olive oil mixing thoroughly to make a paste. The pesto will keep for about a week in the 'fridge in an airtight jar.

Salt the fillets of mackerel and spread a generous layer of pesto on the flesh side.

Preheat a barbecue and carefully place the fillet on

the grill, skin side down. The skin can take a high heat. The fish is cooked once the flesh becomes opaque and flakes, the skin will be chargrilled which adds another dimension to the flavour and is good to eat.

Serve with fresh bread, a green salad and a chilled glass of Sauvignon.

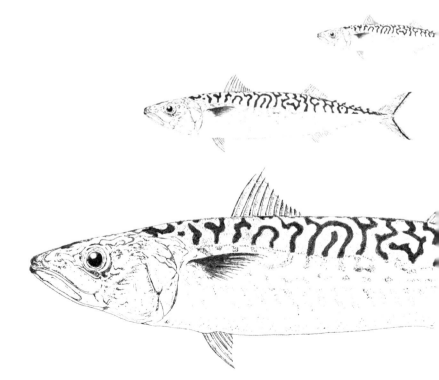

Mackerel cooked in sea water

THIS IS A TERRIFIC way of cooking fresh mackerel which I was told about by a yachtsman. Tastier than ships biscuits with weevils! DM.

1 mackerel per person, depending on size gutted

*but head left on
Seawater*

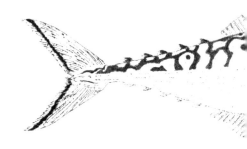

You will need a pan with a close-fitting lid. (I have a shallow round Le Creuset-type one, terribly heavy but works really well.)

Arrange the gutted mackerel in the pan and cover with seawater.

Put on a gentle heat, (on the stove or if you've just caught them, a camp fire) and bring to the boil. Switch off heat or remove from fire and leave for 10 minutes.

The mackerel will be perfectly poached and seasoned. Serve with crusty bread and a chilled glass of white wine.

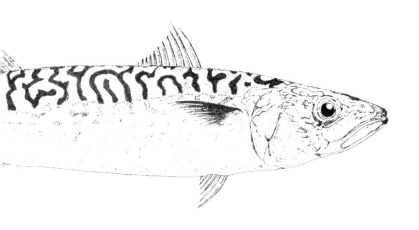

Index

Cook's notes

I like to make notes of how recipes worked for me. I also keep a note of which dishes we serve to which of our friends when they've been in for dinner.